GRAND SLAM

HOPPIE STIBOLT
and
BARBARA BISHOP

Illustrated
by
Katy Murphy Gurtner

Additional copies of GRAND SLAM may be obtained by
sending a check for $10.60 each (Washington state residents add applicable sales tax per book),
plus $1.75 for postage and handling to:
(Make checks out to GRAND SLAM)

GRAND SLAM
2356 Cascade Way
Longview, WA 98632

First Printing   December 1987   10,000 copies

Printed in U.S.A. by
S.C. Toof & Co.
Memphis, TN

INTRODUCTION

This time I am happy to collaborate with my friend of some 30 years, Barbara Bishop, who is known in the northwest for her fabulous cooking. Her expertise and Katy Gurtner's terrific sketches made GRAND SLAM a winning addition to my "Kitchen Sports" trilogy.

Hoppie Stibolt

Cooking has been my pet hobby for many years. I am thrilled to join Hoppie and Katy in my first "Grand Slam" effort.

Barbara Bishop

It's been great fun to do GRAND SLAM as well as the other three cookbooks with Hoppie. We've always perfectly understood each other, have been on the same wavelength. My drawings are the visual expression of her humorous comments.

Katy M. Gurtner

TABLE OF CONTENTS

CARL BORIN

the easy-to-use handbook

BRIDGE
for Bright
Beginners

12-15 points = minimum
16-18 points = good
19+ points = sensational

OPENING BIDS

RESPONSES TO OPENING BIDS

REBIDS BY OPENING BIDDER

DEFENSIVE BIDS

RAISES

NO TRUMP BIDS & RESPONSES

OVERCALLS

TAKE-OUT DOUBLES

PRE-EMPTIVE BIDS

OPENING BIDS

HORS D'OEUVRES

GRAND SLAM SHRIMP DIP

2 1/2 pounds small shrimp, cleaned,
  and cooked
3 8-ounce packages cream cheese,
  room temperature
1/2 cup sour cream
1 1/2 cups mayonnaise
4 green onions — tops and all —
  finely chopped
1/2 cup catsup
1 tablespoon Worcestershire sauce
salt and pepper to taste

Combine ingredients, mix, chill, and
serve with corn chips and crudities.

BASIL DELIGHT

3 cups fresh basil leaves
1 cup parsley
3/4 cup grated Parmesan cheese
2 tablespoons light olive oil
11 ounces softened cream cheese
1/2 cup butter softened
dash salt and lemon juice to taste

Blend until smooth, basil, parsley,
Parmesan cheese, and olive oil.
Combine remaining ingredients and
blend until smooth. In mold, layer basil
mixture, then cheese and repeat 3
times. Chill overnight or a few hours.
Unmold and serve with crackers.

BACON BITES

2 dozen dates, pitted
3 ounces cream cheese
1 pound bacon

Cut bacon slices in half, fry until half cooked (still soft). Drain. Slit dates and fill with a teaspoon of cream cheese. Wrap bacon slices around dates, secure with a toothpick. Bake 15 minutes at 400°.

BLEU CHEESE BITES

4-5 tablespoons Bleu cheese
2 tablespoons butter
4 walnuts chopped fine

Spread on toast rounds. Place under broiler until warm.

FROZEN CHEESE STICKS

1 large loaf white sandwich bread,
  frozen and unsliced
8 ounces cream cheese
1/2 cup butter
1/4 pound sharp Cheddar cheese
1-2 egg whites

Cut frozen bread in 1 1/2″ thick slices, remove crusts and cut each slice in 1 1/2″ squares. Melt cream cheese, butter, and cheddar cheese in top of double broiler, cool; add stiffly beaten egg whites. Dip bread squares into mixture, place on cookie sheet and freeze overnight or longer. Bake still frozen at 350° until brown (about 15-20 minutes). These can be kept in plastic bags several months. Can be used with soups.

KANSAS PRIZE

Soften cream cheese and mix with equal parts of sour cream. Add a can of diced green chilies. Spread on flour tortillas, roll and put in ice box. Can freeze for a week. Cut as for a jelly roll and pinch ends together to make pin wheels. Can also use pimento or chive cream cheese spreads.

SEASONED OYSTER CRACKERS

1 box oyster crackers
1 stick margarine
1 teaspoon seasoning salt
1 1/2 teaspoons garlic salt
1/2 cup Parmesan cheese

Melt margarine, add seasonings, and pour over crackers. Bake at 250° for 45 minutes, stirring occasionally. Can be frozen to have on hand for snacks.

Put these on the corner of your table and you will forget what's trump.

ROSEMARY WALNUTS

1 stick margarine
1 pound walnut halves
2 tablespoons fresh rosemary
1/2 teaspoon cayenne pepper
salt to taste

Heat all in skillet. Adjust seasonings to your taste.

I keep these on hand for drop-in guests. Also tasty sprinkled with Cajun seasoning to taste.

REBID MUNCHIES

2 boxes oyster crackers, butter flavor
1 cup corn oil
2 garlic cloves, crushed
dash dill
1 package Ranch Valley dressing

Mix all together and place in tightly covered container.

BRIDGE NIBBLES

Stuff black and green olives with a smoked oyster.

JAN'S YUM YUM

Serves 10-12

2 cups mayonnaise
2 cups shredded cheese
2 large onions diced
2 drops Worcestershire sauce

Mix and bake at 375° for 20-25 minutes. Serve with crackers.

HOT TACO DIP

1 can condensed bean and bacon
  soup
1 cup sour cream
2 ounces shredded Cheddar cheese
2 tablespoons dry taco seasoning mix
1/2 teaspoon instant minced onion

Combine all ingredients in top of double boiler, mix well and cook uncovered until heated through. Serve with corn or taco chips.

FRIED MOZZARELLA

3 pounds Mozzarella, cut 1" x 4" x 1"
2 cups basil seasoned bread crumbs
1 cup flour
2 eggs beaten
margarine
marinara sauce

Coat the Mozzarella slices with flour, then dip in the beaten egg, and then into the bread crumbs. Chill several hours or overnight in the refrigerator. Fry in the margarine over high heat. If necessary put lid on skillet for 1-2 minutes to make sure the cheese is hot and runny. Slices can be kept warm on paper towels on a baking sheet in a 200° oven. Serve with a marinara tomato sauce for dipping. Can also be made with Brie cheese. Excellent served with a salad course.

MARINARA SAUCE FOR FRIED MOZZARELLA

1/4 cup olive
2 cloves garlic minced
1 tablespoon minced parsley
1 teaspoon basil
dash sugar
2 cups tomatoes
1 teaspoon salt
pepper to taste

Cook garlic and parsley until garlic is lightly browned. Add other ingredients and simmer at least one hour. Store in refrigerator.

DUMMY'S DIP

2 cups chopped fresh mushrooms
2 tablespoons margarine
8 slices bacon
4 tablespoons onion
6 ounces cream cheese
2 tablespoons sour cream
2 tablespoons sherry or to taste
salt to taste

Sauté mushrooms in margarine. Fry bacon until crisp; crumble. Sauté onion in a little bacon fat, then combine onion, bacon and mushrooms. Stir in cream cheese softened with sour cream and sherry. Serve on Triskets or Benne wafers. Can be used for sandwich spread.

My friend said no one would eat these — too hot. Wrong! Put close to the bar.

TEXAS PEANUTS

2 tablespoons vegetable oil
4 garlic cloves, minced
1 tablespoon dried red pepper flakes
2 pounds salted peanuts
1 teaspoon chili powder

Preheat oven to 350°. Heat oil in large skillet over medium heat. Add garlic and pepper flakes. Cook 1 minute. Add peanuts and stir. Transfer to baking sheet and bake until slightly brown — about 10 minutes. Sprinkle with chili powder, toss, and cool completely. Store in air tight containers at least 8 hours. Makes about 6 cups.

POTATO SKINS

6 potatoes
4 tablespoons butter
2 teaspoons Worcestershire sauce
2 teaspoons minced garlic

Bake potatoes and cut in quarters lengthwise. Scoop out center, leaving 1/4" shell. Let dry on baking sheet 1 hour. Melt butter with Worcestershire sauce, garlic, salt and pepper and brush skin on both sides. Bake 10 minutes or until crisp at 500°. Serve with extras, such as chives, sour cream, bacon, guacamole, and shredded Cheddar cheese.

CRANBERRY CANAPE

Cover cream cheese with cranberry chutney and serve on Wheat Thins.

CRANBERRY CHUTNEY

1/2 cup cider vinegar
2 1/4 cups brown sugar
1 teaspoon curry powder
1/2 teaspoon ginger
1/4 teaspoon cloves
1/4 teaspoon allspice
1/2 teaspoon cinnamon
2 lemons, rind and wedges
1 apple
1 1/2 cups raisins
1/2 cup dried apricots
1/2 cup walnuts
1 1/2 cups water
2 pounds cranberries

Place cranberries in a large saucepan with water to cover. Bring to a boil, then simmer 5 minutes or until berries pop. Add remaining ingredients except nuts. Cook on low heat about 30 minutes. Remove from heat and add nuts. Pour into hot sterilized jars. Fill to top and seal at once. Use with cream cheese hors d'oeuvres or serve with chicken.

NUTTY DIP

1 cup salted peanuts, chopped
2 1/4 cups mayonnaise
3 teaspoons curry powder
6 tablespoons chopped chutney
1 1/4 cups coconut
1 cup pineapple, drained and cut up

Mix ingredients and chill. Serve in a hollowed out pineapple with celery, carrot sticks, mushrooms and peppers.

CHEESE-NUT BALL

8 ounces cream cheese
4 cloves mashed garlic
1 5-ounce can evaporated milk
1 pound grated Cheddar cheese
3/4 cup chopped pitted ripe olives
2 cups chopped pecans
4 dashes Tabasco sauce
1/2 teaspoon paprika
salt to taste

Soften cream cheese, and blend in garlic, milk and cheese. Mix in remaining ingredients except paprika and chill. Make a ball or 3-4 rolls and sprinkle with paprika. Wrap in foil until needed. Can also be used for cheese bread, and or sandwiches.

CAVIAR SPREAD

8 ounces cream cheese
4 hard-cooked eggs, chopped
4-5 green onions, chopped
6 ounces sour cream
4 ounces caviar

Layer the ingredients in an 8″ round serving dish. Serve with toast rounds.

BAKED WHOLE BRIE OR CAMEMBERT

1. Brush any size cheese with butter and brown sugar. Arrange chopped pecans or walnuts on top. Bake in 350° oven until cheese begins to melt — 10-12 minutes. Serve with bread sticks or apple wedges or Wheat Thins.

2. Let cheese stand at room temperature for 15 minutes. Beat one egg until blended. Coat cheese with flour, egg and seasoned herb bread crumbs. Chill overnight. Melt 3 tablespoons margarine or butter in a frying pan over medium heat. When pan is hot, add cheese and cook until golden on bottom — 1-2 minutes. Lightly brown other side 1/2-1 minute longer. Garnish with chives. Serve on crackers or toasted baguette slices.

3. Heat until soft and almost runny in a microwave oven — 2-3 minutes.

SINGLETON DIP

3/4 cup sesame seeds
1/2 pound Bleu cheese
1 pound cream cheese
1/2 cup margarine
1 cup chopped pimento green olives
1 tablespoon chopped chives
1 tablespoon chopped parsley
1/2 teaspoon garlic salt
3 tablespoon cognac

Roast sesame seeds in shallow pan at 350° for 20 minutes — be careful not to burn. Cream cheeses and margarine, and add rest of the ingredients and blend. Roll in sesame seeds and serve with crackers.

CHICKEN LIVER PATE

1 1/2 pounds chicken livers
3/4 pound sliced bacon
2 small onions
6 garlic cloves
6 bay leaves
1 1/2 teaspoons salt
1/4 - 1/2 teaspoon red pepper
3 tablespoons Worcestershire sauce
3/4 teaspoon nutmeg
1 1/2 teaspoons mustard
1/4 teaspoon cloves

Wash livers, put in a covered pan with cut-up bacon, bay leaves, onion, garlic, salt, pepper and Worcestershire sauce. Boil for 20 minutes in just enough water to cover. When done discard bay leaves and all but about 1/4 cup of the liquid — just enough to make a thick pate. Add remaining ingredients, blend and put in mold. Will keep in refrigerator a week — 6 months in the freezer.

BANKER'S OYSTERS

Roll oysters in beaten egg, then in touch of bread crumbs. Put a splash of vermouth over each and bake next to broiler until brown.

100 HONORS COCKTAIL MEATBALLS

1/2 pound ground beef
1/2 pound ground pork
1/2 pound ground veal
1 cup finely chopped onion
2 eggs
1 cup seasoned bread crumbs
2 cloves finely chopped garlic
1/4 cup chopped parsley
1 tablespoon minced fresh mint, if
  available

Mix all ingredients together and shape into meatballs. Place on cookie sheet and bake 20-25 minutes at 350°, or on high power microwave for 12 minutes. Can be frozen — reheat before serving. Serve with Chili California sauce.

CHILI CALIFORNIA SAUCE

1/2 cup olive oil
3 cloves minced garlic
1/2 cup red wine
1/8 cup tomato paste
1/2 cup lemon juice
1/4 cup minced fresh basil
1 chopped hot chili pepper

Combine all ingredients and simmer about 10 minutes.

LOOKS LIKE SHRIMP

1/2 pound sliced dried beef
8 ounces cream cheese
1 teaspoon Worcestershire sauce
2 teaspoons prepared horseradish
1/2 teaspoon onion salt
2 tablespoons lemon juice or dry
  sherry

Combine cream cheese, Worcestershire sauce, horseradish, onion, salt, and lemon juice. Blend until creamy. Spread cheese on dried beef slices and roll up each jelly roll fashion. Chill well in foil wrap. Cut in bite-sized pieces. Spear each with cocktail pick.

This is a good first course also.

NANCY'S SHRIMP

Shell, devein, and butterfly 4 large shrimp per person. Dip in melted butter, then in fresh bread crumbs that have been mixed with fresh basil, salt, pepper, and cayenne. Lay flat with tail over the top on a tray. Bake at 500° for 5 minutes. Serve plain, or with a cocktail sauce or with guacamole.

Good done outside on grill.

BARBECUED PRAWNS

1 pound prawns in shells
1 cup olive oil
1/2 cup picked cilantro leaves
2 cloves garlic
juice of 2 limes
1/2 teaspoon salt
1/2 teaspoon pepper

Mix all ingredients except prawns in cuisinart or blender. Marinate prawns at least 2 hours (overnight is better) in the mixture. Thread on skewers and barbeque about 2 minutes per side. Shell and enjoy.

The hit of the party!

ONE-EYED JACK OR STUFFED CHEESE

1/2 pound ground beef
4 ounce can chopped green chilies,
  drained
2 1/4 ounce can black chopped olives
1 diced tomato
2 pounds Jack cheese
chili powder, salt and garlic powder to
  taste
salsa

Brown beef, drain. Stir in chilies, olives, tomato, chili powder, salt and garlic powder. Simmer 10 minutes. Hollow out cheese, leaving a 1/2″ shell. Fill cheese with meat mixture and place in a close-fitting casserole dish. Bake uncovered at 350° for 10 minutes or until cheese begins to melt and is soft. Spoon salsa over it and serve with chips.

VULNERABLE

DRINKS

This is a tradition in our family at Christmas time, and the first time I have shared this recipe.

CHOCOLATE EGGNOG

Serves 20-30

3 quarts eggnog, chilled
1 can chocolate syrup
2 cups rum
1/2 ounce grated semisweet
  chocolate, grated for garnish

Combine in large punch bowl.

GIBSON BOWL

Serves 30

3 limes, cut in thin slices
1/2 cup sugar
1/4 cup water
2 fifths of vodka
2 cups Roses lime juice

Mix and chill.

LITTLE SLAM

Serves 4

1 large can frozen limeade
1 can vodka
1 can water
ice cubes

Blend in blender.

HURRICANES

Serves 2

4 ounces rum (half dark, half golden)
4 ounces Hurricane mix

Mix and serve over ice.

BAILEY'S FIZZ

Serves one

Won't you come home Bill Baily?
Mix equal parts Baileys Irish Ceam and club soda. Serve over ice in a tall glass.

AMARETTO COOLER

Serves 1

1 jigger of amaretto
quinine water
lime
ice

Add a jigger of amaretto to a glass, and fill with quinine water and a squirt of fresh lime.

ORANGE CHAMPAGNE COCKTAIL PUNCH

Serves 20

2 bottles champagne
1 quart of gingerale
2 cups orange juice

Serve in glasses with a few strawberry slices.

Great for a winter's evening bridge party.

ORANGE-BRANDY PUNCH

Serves 24

8 oranges, cut in half and studded
   with cloves
1/2 gallon cider
1 quart apple brandy
pinch cinnamon
pinch allspice
pinch nutmeg

Place in large pot and heat until hot.

GODFATHER

1/3 amaretto
2/3 scotch

Serves 1

Blend and serve over ice. Can be made half and half if you prefer.

ATHOLE BROZE

1 part honey
2 parts cream
3 parts scotch

Single serving

Heat together and serve in a stemmed glass.

You lead through strength with this drink.

EL PRESIDENTE

1/3 jigger Curacao or Grand Marnier
1 jigger gold rum
1 1/3 jigger dry vermouth
dash grenadine

Shake with ice and serve.

Single serving

DON'S RED ONION

2 parts gin
1 part pernod
1 ounce grenadine

Serve on ice.

MEDITERRANEAN STINGER

2 parts lemon juice
1 part Curacao
3 parts gin

Serve on ice.

Serves 2

FROZEN PEACH DAIQUIRIS

Serves 4

2 large peaches, peeled and sliced
1 tablespoon lemon juice
4-6 ounces light or dark rum
juice of one lime
4 cubes ice

Put all ingredients in a blender and blend until smooth. Place in freezer until frosty.

KIWI DAIQUIRIES

Serves 4

2 kiwi fruit, pared and quartered
4 teaspoons sugar
2 tablespoons lime juice
2-4 jiggers rum
10 ice cubes

Place all ingredients in a blender and puree until smooth.

Courtesy of the good doctor in Chanute.

MY FAVORITE MINT JULEP

Serves one

Bruise 30-40 mint leaves in 4 teaspoons sugar in an old-fashioned glass. Dilute with water to fill glass. In julep glass fill with crushed ice and 1 jigger of mint syrup mix. Fill to the top with bourbon — 3-4 ounces. Stir with silver spoon until outside is frosted. Decorate with sprig of mint, powdered sugar, and 2 straws. As you drink, add more bourbon and put down your cards.

HOT TODDY

2 teaspoons sugar
juice of 1/2 lemon
1 teaspoon Curacao
2 jiggers rum

Heat in pan. Serve in a stemmed glass.

BELLINI

1 bottle of dry champagne
2 large ripe peaches
juice of one orange
juice of one lemon
4 tablespoons Creme de Cassis

Pureé the peaches and add lemon and orange juice and Cassis. Mix 1/3 bellini with 2/3 champagne and serve in champagne glasses. Ciav! This reminds me of a sunny day in Venice, thanks to Hoppie and Carl.

HONORS

SOUPS, SANDWICHES & LUNCH DISHES

MEXICAN STYLE OYSTER CHOWDER

Serves 4

1 onion
2 cloves garlic
1 yellow pepper
1 broccoli top (6-8 flowerettes)
3 cups clam juice
1/2 cup chopped, peeled, skinned
  tomatoes
4 tablespoons salsa
2 dozen small oysters
1 teaspoon oregano and cayenne to
  taste
cilantro, scallion tops, sour cream

Sauté onions, garlic and peppers. Add clam broth, tomato and broccoli, salsa and seasonings. Simmer 10 minutes. Add oysters and continue to cook until they are plump. Serve with spoonful of sour cream, scallion tops and cilantro sprigs.

OYSTER MUSHROOM SOUP

2 tablespoons margarine
3 medium onions, chopped
1 pound oyster mushrooms, sliced
3 cups chicken bouillon
1/2 cup chopped parsley
1 minced garlic clove
1/4 teaspoon pepper
1/2 cup dry white wine

Melt margarine and sauté onions until tender. Add mushrooms and lightly saute. Stir in other ingredients except wine. Bring to boil, reduce heat and add wine. Simmer 5 minutes. Can garnish with croutons, Parmesan cheese and/or parsley.

MUSHROOM SOUP

Serves 4

1 pound mushrooms, chopped
2 tablespoons sugar
6 tablespoons margarine
1 finely chopped onion
1/4 cup flour
1 pint Half and Half
1 can chicken broth
1/2 cup dry vermouth
salt and pepper to taste

Sauté onions until golden. Add sugar and cook 1 more minute. Add mushrooms and sauté 5 minutes. Stir in flour until smooth; cook 2 minutes. Pour in Half and Half, stir; add remaining ingredients and heat to boiling, stirring constantly. Reduce heat and simmer 10 minutes.

BACHELOR BRIDGE SOUP

Serves 12

3 ham hocks
2 quarts water
2 large onions, chopped
1 large smoked sausage, sliced
4-6 cloves garlic, minced
3 large potatoes, peeled and diced
3 sliced carrots
6 chopped tomatoes
1 13-ounce can tomato sauce
1 large bunch watercress, cut in
  pieces (optional)
4 cups canned kidney beans
basil, bay leaf, salt and pepper to
  taste

Simmer ham hocks 2 hours, cool and remove meat from bones. Give the bones to the dog and set the meat aside. To the broth, add onion, sausage, garlic, potatoes, carrots, tomatoes and seasonings. Simmer 45 minutes. Add tomato sauce, watercress, beans and ham pieces. Simmer until heated through.

WINTER STEAK SOUP

Serves 12-16

1 pound ground beef, brown and drain
2 pound can stewed tomatoes
1 pound can tomato sauce
4 cups water
1 teaspoon Mexican seasoning
20 ounce package frozen mixed vegetables
1 package Lipton onion soup mix
2 teaspoons sugar
1 small can sliced water chestnuts
1 small can sliced mushrooms

Add all ingredients to browned and drained beef. Simmer at least one hour.

SOUP FOR A GROUP

Serves 30+

9 quarts water
3 pounds beef
1 shank soup bone
1 bunch celery
1 whole onion
3 tablespoons Lawry's salt
1 teaspoon garlic salt
1 1/2 teaspoon basil
1 teaspoon chervil
1 teaspoon thyme
1 teaspoon oregano
1 tablespoon pepper
2 tablespoons sugar

Cover beef and soup bone and simmer 3 1/2 hours. Remove meat and trim off fat. Strain broth, skim fat and return to pot and add: 8-10 carrots, 1 bunch green onions, celery, 1 package each of peas, cauliflower, corn, green beans, lima beans and okra, (10-ounce packages), 1 2 1/2-ounce can tomatoes, 1 2 1/2-ounce can tomato juice. Add all but the frozen ingredients and cook uncovered 1/2 hour. Add frozen vegetables and remove from heat. Refrigerate. Before reheating, skim off the fat.

ASPARAGUS SOUP

Serves 2

1 small chopped onion
1 1/2 tablespoons unsalted butter
2 cups chicken broth
1 pound asparagus, cut in 1" pieces
1/4 cup sour cream

Sauté onion in butter. Add broth and asparagus and bring to a boil. Cook 2 minutes. Pureé in blender and add sour cream. Return to burner and heat. Do not boil.

CREAM OF SHRIMP SOUP WITH BASIL

Serves 6

3 cups sliced mushrooms
1/4 cup sliced scallions
1 clove garlic, minced
2 tablespoons butter
2 cups hot chicken broth
1/2 cup dry sherry
1 cup chiffinade of fresh basil
14 ounces fresh or frozen shelled
  shrimp
2 cups cream
3 egg yoks

Sauté vegetables in butter until tender but not brown. Add chicken broth, 1 cup cream and shrimp. Heat to boiling and simmer until shrimp are hot — about 3 minutes. Mix remaining cup of cream with egg yolks and add to broth with basil. Heat and stir just until thickened, but do not allow to boil.

TURKEY SOUP

Serves 6-8

3 cups broth with giblets
4+ cups turkey
1/4 cup long grain rice
2 bunches green onions
1 can cream of celery soup
1 can cream of mushroom soup
poultry seasoning
herb seasoning

Throw everything into a pot and simmer all day or at least 4 hours. This is great for leftover Christmas turkey, so cook your turkey giblets in lots of water.

LETTUCE SOUP

Serves 4

1 10 3/4-ounce can chicken broth
1/2 teaspoon dried thyme
10 cups torn leaf lettuce
4 tablespoons chives
2 tablespoons margarine
2 tablespoons flour
1/8 teaspoon salt and pepper
1 cup light cream or 1 cup liquid non-
  dairy coffee cream
sour cream

Bring broth and thyme to boiling, add lettuce and cover. Cook 3 minutes or until wilted. Remove and cool. Blend in cuisinart. Cook chives; add flour, salt and pepper, then cream. Cook until thickened. Stir into lettuce mixture with 3-4 tablespoons of sour cream. Heat and serve. Top with dab of sour cream. Serve hot or cold.

STRAWBERRY SOUP

3 pints fresh strawberries
2 1/2 cups orange juice
1/4 cup Grand Marnier liqueur
sugar to taste

Pureé berries until smooth. Pour in large bowl and add other ingredients. Chill 1 hour. Serve with sliced strawbeerries and a dab of sour cream or Creme Fraiche on top if desired. See page 122 for Creme Fraiche recipe.

CARROT AND TOMATO SOUP

Serves 6-8

1 chopped onion
3 cups peeled and sliced carrots
3 chopped tomatoes (2 if large)
1 cup chopped celery
2 chopped leeks — white ends only
1/2 cup unsalted butter
2 heavy dashes thyme
5 cups chicken stock
1/2 cup heavy cream — optional
salt and pepper to taste

Sauté onions, carrots, tomatoes, celery and leeks in butter 5 minutes; add seasonings and chicken stock and simmer about 20 minutes. Pureé in small batches until smooth. Add cream and chill. Serve with croutons or crisp pita.

ICED TOMATO SOUP

Serves 2

Chop 1 large can stewed tomatoes into small pieces. Mix with 1 grated onion, salt and pepper. Put in freezer. When well chilled, stir in 1 tablespoon mayonnaise and curry powder.

CROSS RUFF GAZPACHO

1 clove garlic
2 teaspoons salt
1/2 cup chopped mushrooms
3 tablespoons olive oil
1 cup chopped green onions, tops
  also
2 cups finely chopped tomatoes
1 cup finely chopped green peppers
1 cup chopped cucumber
1 cup chopped celery
1 tablespoon chopped chives
2 tablespoons chopped parsley
1 teaspoon freshly ground pepper
Tabasco sauce to taste (1/2 to 1
  teaspoon)
2 teaspoons Worcestershire sauce
1/2 cup tarragon wine vinegar
3 cups V-8 Tomato Juice

Crush garlic in the salt. Sauté mushrooms in olive oil until lightly browned. Combine all the ingredients, cover, and chill 3 hours or overnight.

SUMMER FUN SOUP

Serves 6

1/4 cup unsalted butter
3 chopped pears
1 10-ounce package frozen peas,
  thawed
1 cup chopped onion
4 leeks (use white-end up to pale
  green)
2 peeled and chopped red potatoes
4 cups chicken stock
1/2 cup whipping cream, if desired
salt and pepper to taste

In large frying pan, sauté pears, onion, leeks, and potato in melted butter 15 minutes. Add chicken stock and simmer 15 minutes more. Add peas and cook another five minutes. Add salt and pepper to taste. Pureé in small batches until smooth. Place in serving bowls and swish in cream. Chill several hours. Good served with crispy pita.

SANDWICH TRUMPS

Single serving

1 slice ham
1 slice Swiss cheese
1 slice chicken
2 slices bread
2 eggs
1/8 cup Half and Half

Beat eggs with Half and Half, and put sandwich in mixture until absorbed. Fry lightly in butter until cheese starts to melt. Yum!

TUNA SPREAD

1 can tuna fish, drained
3 ounces cream cheese
1/4 cup sherry
2 tablespoons minced parsley
2 tablespoons minced chives
1/4 teaspoon tarragon
sour cream or mayonnaise
dash seasoning salt

Combine all ingredients, adding enough sour cream to make a spreading consistency. Add salt to taste. Can also add capers and/or nuts. May be used as a dip.

CHILI SANDWICH LOAF

Serves 8-10

1 large unsliced sandwich loaf

Remove crusts and cut into 4 slices lengthwise. Butter top of each. Fill one layer with ham salad, next with egg salad, next with chicken salad. Press together and cover the top and sides with cream cheese mixed with 2 teaspoons chili powder. Decorate with olives, green pepper, and pimento. These are basic fillings — use your own ideas. How about a Mexican one with guacamole, sliced olives mixed with mayonnaise and a jalapeno cheese mixture? Put green chilies in the cream cheese that covers the bread. Ole!

SHRIMP REMOULADE *For a light lunch*

Serves 4

2 pounds of cooked and deveined shrimp
1/2 cup lemon juice
1/2 cup tarragon vinegar
6 tablespoons mustard
1 tablespoon horseradish
4 teaspoons paprika
2 cups light olive oil
2 cups chopped celery
1 cup chopped green onion
salt and pepper to taste

Mix all ingredients, except shrimp. Marinate shrimp in liquid 4 hours.

I can understand why Bill likes this.

SHRIMPS WITH GARLIC AND HERBS

Serves 6

2 cloves garlic, minced
1 teaspoon of finely minced parsley
1 teaspoon scallions
1 teaspoon shallots
1 teaspoon chives
1 teaspoon chervil
1 teaspoon tarragon
1 teaspoon thyme
1/4 pound butter
2 cups fresh bread crumbs
1/4 cup dry sherry
dash tabasco sauce
pinch nutmeg
pinch mace
salt and pepper to taste
2 pounds uncooked jumbo shrimp

Stir minced garlic and herbs together and blend with butter. Reduce to 1/2 teaspoon if using dried herbs. Add bread crumbs, sherry, tabasco, mace, nutmeg, salt and pepper. Put in refrigerator several hours or even the day before to blend flavors. Bring pot of water to a boil with 1 package of shrimp or crab boil spices. Add shrimp and when the water returns to boil cook only 3 minutes and drain. Shell shrimp. Put half of bread mixture into a flat 8" x 10" casserole. Make one layer of shrimp and sprinkle with remaining half of crumbs. Bake in preheated oven 400° for 10-15 minutes or 10 minutes and then under the broiler to brown tops. Good with green salad and toasted English muffins.

STUFFED ARTICHOKES

Serves 6

Boil 6 artichokes in salted water 20-30 minutes or until tender. Drain and cool. When cool remove center leaves and choke. Fill with stuffing of your choice.

Scallop-olive stuffing:
1 pound bay scallops
2 tablespoons margarine
12 chopped stuffed olives
1 tablespoon olive oil
2 tablespoons white wine
4 tablespoons chopped parsley or any
  fresh herb
juice of 1/2 lime

Sauté scallops in butter and wine 5 minutes. Add salt and pepper to taste. Remove from heat and add rest of ingredients. Toss well. Can uses shrimp instead of scallops.

BROCCOLI CHICKEN CASSEROLE

Serves 6

3 chicken breasts
1 cup broccoli flowerettes
1 can cream of mushroom soup
1/2 can chicken broth
2 teaspoons curry powder
1 teaspoon lemon juice
3/4 cup mayonnaise
shredded Cheddar cheese
basil bread crumbs

Cook chicken until tender; bone and place in 8" x 8" casserole. Add chopped broccoli. Combine soups, curry, lemon juice and mayonnaise. Pour over broccoli. Sprinkle with cheese and bread crumbs and top with paprika. Bake at 350° for 30-35 minutes. Can be frozen and reheated in microwave.

DON'S CASSEROLE FOR THE GIRLS

Serves 4

2 cups broccoli flowerettes
1 cup ham cubes
4 ounces cream cheese
4 ounces Bleu cheese
8 ounces rotini, cooked al dente
2 cups evaporated milk
2 tablespoons margarine
Italian seasoning
pepper
Parmesan cheese

Cook broccoli 5-7 minutes and drain. Heat milk and margarine. Crumble in cheeses and stir until cheese is melted and sauce is thick. Add broccoli, ham, and warm pasta. Season with pinch of Italian seasoning, and pinch of pepper. Turn into individual serving dishes and top with Parmesan cheese and parsley. Casserole may be made in advance, refrigerated, and heated to serving temperature in oven or microwave just before serving.

GREEN CHILI QUICHE

Serves 4

7 ounce can chopped green chilies
3/4 pound grated sharp Cheddar
  cheese
4 eggs
salt and pepper to taste
2-3 drops tabasco sauce, to taste

Line bottom and sides of a 9″ pie plate with chilies. Sprinkle cheese over peppers. Beat eggs with seasoning. Pour over cheese and chilies. Top with paprika. Bake at 350° for 25-30 minutes. Slice into wedges. Pass salsa. Could be an appetizer or side dish.

LEEK, MUSHROOM AND SPINACH STRATA

Serves 12

16 slices of sourdough French bread
2 tablespoons margarine
2 cups sliced leeks
1/2 pound mushrooms, sliced
1/4 cup dry sherry
1 1/4 teaspoons salt
3 chicken breast halves, cooked and
  chopped
1 packed cup of fresh spinach leaves,
  shredded
2 teaspoons dry basil
3 cups shredded sharp Cheddar
  cheese
8 eggs
2 cups light cream
2 cups milk

Cut bread into 1 1/2" squares. Grease 10" x 13" pan on bottom and sides. Line bottom of pan with half the bread squares. In skillet, melt margarine; add leeks and mushrooms and sauté until juice from mushrooms evaporates. Add sherry and half the salt; cook until sherry evaporates. Remove from heat and stir in chicken, spinach, basil and spread over bread. Top with 2 cups of cheese and remaining bread. Beat eggs; add cream, milk and remaining salt. Spoon over bread mixture. Sprinkle with last cup of cheese; cover with foil and refrigerate overnight. May be made 24 hours in advance. Bake in 350° oven for 40-60 minutes, until golden and puffed and egg mixture is set.

HAM PASTA BRUNCH

1/2 pound linguine
1/2 pound thinly sliced baked ham
1/3 cup Bleu cheese, crumbled
2 cups walnut pieces
1 cup parsley
1/4 cup chopped fresh rosemary
2 cloves minced garlic
1 1/2 teaspoons pepper
1 cup olive oil or walnut oil

Combine all ingredients except linguine. Stir and let stand covered at room temperature for 4 hours. Cook pasta, drain, and immediately toss with sauce. Spinach angel hair pasta used for testing. Delicious!

PASTA WITH PARSLEY PESTO

Serves 4

4 cups parsley
1 cup pine nuts
1 cup Parmesan cheese
1 cup olive oil
4 cloves minced garlic
salt, to taste
1/4 cup margarine
1 tablespoon minced dill
1 pint cherry tomatoes
1 pound of pasta, your choice

In food processor, make pesto of parsley, nuts, cheese, oil, garlic, and salt. Sauté dill and tomatoes in margarine. Arrange hot pasta on platter, put pesto on top and tomatoes on top or sides.

NO TRUMP PASTA

Serves 6

1/2 pound broccoli flowerettes
2 cups mushrooms, sliced
1 red bell pepper, sliced
1 pint cherry tomatoes, halved
4 ounces salami, cut in strips
3/4 pound fettuccine
1 cup fresh Parmesan cheese, grated
3 cloves garlic
1/4 cup cream
pesto sauce, to taste

Blanch broccoli; sauté garlic in margarine and add mushrooms, red pepper and broccoli. When hot, add tomatoes and salami. Cook pasta al dente, drain, and toss with pesto sauce and cream. Add vegetables and toss. Sprinkle with fresh Parmesan cheese. See page 60 for Pesto Sauce.

FOUR HEARTS PASTA

Serves 8

1 pound fusilli
1/2 green pepper, cut in thin strips
1/2 red pepper, cut in thin strips
1/2 pound mushrooms, sliced
1 cup broccoli flowerettes
1 small zucchini, sliced
1 6-ounce jar marinated artichoke
  hearts
1 1/2 teaspoons olive oil
1/2-1 cup pesto sauce

Prepare pasta to "al dente." Sauté peppers in oil until soft and remove. Stir fry mushrooms until slightly cooked; remove. Stir fry broccoli 1-2 minutes; remove. Add zucchini and cook until crisp. Put all in bowl and add undrained artichoke hearts. Season with salt and pepper to taste. Combine pasta, vegetables, and pesto sauce. Garnish with fresh basil leaves.

GREEK PASTA CLUB LUNCH

Serves 8

1/4 cup olive oil
1/4 cup tarragon vinegar
8 ounces Feta cheese
1 tablespoon oregano
1/4 teaspoon garlic powder
1 pound fettucini, cooked al dente
1/2 cup chopped cucumbers
1/2 cup chopped tomatoes
1/2 cup chopped red onion
1/4 cup chopped black Greek olives

Combine first five ingredients and marinate the cooked pasta overnight in the refrigerator. Just before serving, add vegetables. Add more oil and vinegar if necessary. Garnish with olives.

CHICKEN TRUMPED WITH ARTICHOKES AND MUSHROOMS   *Serves 6-8*

4 whole boned chicken breasts
2 cups artichoke hearts, drained
3/4 pound sliced sautéed mushrooms

White Sauce:
1/4 cup margarine
1/3 cup flour
1/2 cup white wine
3 cups chicken stock
salt and pepper to taste

Brown chicken breasts in margarine and garlic salt — if you like that flavor. Layer in casserole with artichoke hearts and mushrooms in middle layer. Pour white sauce on top and cover; bake at 350° for 1 hour. This is another do ahead to warm later in microwave.

BRIDGE CHICKEN   *Serves 6*

6 chicken breasts, skinned
1 bottle of Russian salad dressing
1 package Lipton's onion soup mix
1 jar of chutney — any kind

Grease baking dish. Dip chicken breasts in Russian dressing and put in dish. Place onion soup mix on top of breasts and then chutney on top of that. Bake at 300° for 1 1/2 hours. Can be cooked earlier and reheated in the microwave.

PINEAPPLE TURKEY CURRY SALAD

Serves 4-6

4 cups diced turkey
1 can sliced, drained water chestnuts
1 1/2 cups grapes, sliced
1 cup sliced celery
1/2 cup toasted slivered almonds

Combine.

1 1/2 cups mayonnaise
2 tablespoons curry powder
2 teaspoons soy sauce
1 can sliced pineapple, drained

Blend mayonnaise, curry, and soy sauce and 2 teaspoons pineapple juice. Combine with turkey. Serve on pineapple slices and lettuce.

NANCY'S FANCY

Serves 4-6

4 chicken breasts, cooked and cut up
2 cups Chinese pea pods, blanched and drained
1 box 10-ounce frozen peas, thawed
1 box cherry tomatoes, halved
1 cup chopped celery
1 cup chopped green onions
1 cup cooked spiral macaroni shells
1/2 cup mayonnaise
1/2 cup sour cream

Mix together and chill overnight or for a few hours. Add more mayonnaise if necessary.

CURRY TURKEY

Serves 6-8

1/4 cup margarine
2 cups diced celery
2 cups chopped onions
4 cups milk
1/4 cup flour
2 envelopes chicken bouillon
2 tablespoons curry powder or to
taste
1 5 3/4-ounce can pitted ripe olives,
halved and drained
4 cups sliced cooked turkey or
chicken

Cook celery and onion in margarine until limp. Stir in flour, salt, bouillon and curry. Heat, stirring until blended. Slowly stir in milk and cook over medium heat until thickened. Stir in olives and turkey. Serve over toast points, Chinese noodles, or English muffins for lunch or brunch.

BRUNCH CLUB EGGS

Serves 12-15

2 dozen eggs
1 tablespoon parsley
1 cup milk
salt and pepper
1 can cream of mushroom soup
1 carton sour cream
1 pound bacon, fried and crumbled
8 ounces jalapeno cheese, shredded
fresh mushrooms, sliced and cooked

Scramble eggs with milk, parsley, salt, and pepper. Mix soup and sour cream. Spread soup mixture over cooked eggs in a 9" x 13" dish. Put bacon on top, then mushrooms and cheese. Bake at 325° for 30-40 minutes. Can be made the night before.

SPINACH LASAGNE

1 pound lean ground chuck
1 medium onion, chopped
2 cloves garlic
6 ounce can tomato paste
1 20-ounce can tomatoes
1/2 teaspoon salt
1/4 teaspoon pepper
1 teaspoon oregano
1 teaspoon basil
1/2 pound mozzarella cheese
12 ounce low-fat cottage cheese
1/2 cup Parmesan cheese
2 packages frozen chopped spinach,
  thawed
8 ounce package cooked lasagna
  noodles
dash hot sauce

Brown chuck, onion, and garlic. Drain. Add tomato paste, tomatoes and seasonings and simmer until thickened. Combine cheeses and spinach. In a 9″ x 12″ casserole, layer noodles, meat sauce and cheese mixture. Repeat, ending with cheese. Bake uncovered 350° for 30-35 minutes. Good for supper too!

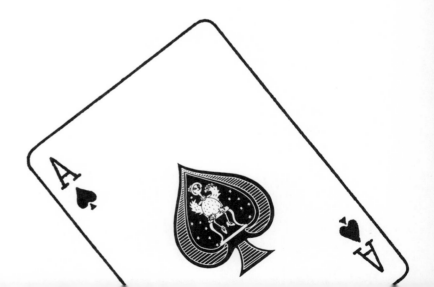

HONEYMOON BRIDGE LUNCH

3 cups cooked turkey
1 cup sliced celery
1/3 cup sliced green onion
2/3 cup toasted chopped walnuts,
  toasted until golden brown.

Curried Bleu Cheese Dressing:
1 cup mayonnaise
2 1/2 tablespoons crumbled Bleu
  cheese
1 tablespoon lemon juice
salt
1/2 teaspoon curry powder

Mix.
Good with crispy herbed pita bread.

CHICKEN-SPINACH WONTONS

Serves 4

1 cup chicken
1 cup spinach
1/2 cup Parmesan cheese
garlic
salt and pepper
nutmeg
mayonnaise, if necessary
1 package wontons

Grind ingredients in food processor. Cut wontons diagonally and wet long edge. Starting at small end, put in a teaspoon of the mixture and roll. Seal ends. Drop in salted boiling water. Boil about 20 minutes, until they come to the top. Serve with white sauce made with cream cheese and sherry.

WELSH RAREBIT

Serves 4-6

1 pound grated sharp Cheddar
 cheese
4 tablespoons butter
1 1/2 cups milk
4 eggs
1 tablespoon mustard
2 tablespoons Worcestershire sauce
salt, pepper, paprika to taste

In double broiler, put cheese, butter and milk; stir. Add eggs, Worcestershire sauce, mustard, salt and pepper and stir over low heat until thick. Pour over toast or English muffins. An oldie, but a goodie.

BRUNCH EGGS

Serves 6

8 slices bacon, diced
2 tablespoons margarine
2 1/2 ounces dried beef, shredded
1/2 pound sliced fresh mushrooms
1/4 cup flour
2 cups milk
1/4 teaspoon pepper
8 eggs
1/2 teaspoon salt
1/2 cup evaporated milk
2 tablespoons margarine
1 cup shredded Cheddar cheese

Cook bacon until crisp, drain. Add margarine, dried beef and mushrooms to the bacon and cook until mushrooms are done. Add flour, stirring constantly, and cook 2 minutes. Add 2 cups of milk and pepper; cook until thick and smooth, stirring constantly. Mix the eggs with salt and evaporated milk. Soft scramble eggs in 2 tablespoons margarine. Put a small amount of the sauce in buttered 9″ x 9″ baking dish. Layer eggs and remaining sauce and cheese. Bake uncovered at 275° for 1 hour. Can be prepared up to two days ahead. Cover and refrigerate until ready to bake. Great for brunch for weekend guests also.

SOMETHING SPECIAL

Serves 8-10

1 1/2 dozen hard-boiled eggs, sliced
  thinly
1/2 pound crisp bacon, crumbled
2 cans mushroom soup
1 cup milk
1 1/2 cups grated Cheddar cheese
1/2 teaspoon marjoram
1/2 teaspoon thyme
1/2 teaspoon basil
1/4 cup chopped parsley
salt and pepper to taste

Mix soup, milk and cheese until melted. Mix seasonings and add to mixture. Layer eggs, bacon, and sauce in casserole. Bake at 350° for 20 minutes. Serve on toast or toasted English muffins.

SPINACH AND CHEESE PIE

Serves 6

1 pie crust
2 tablespoons pine nuts
2 tablespoons salad oil
1/2 pound mushrooms, sliced
1 onion, thinly sliced
3/4 teaspoon savory
1/4 teaspoon pepper
10 ounces spinach, frozen or fresh
4 eggs
1/2 cup milk
1/2 pound shredded Swiss cheese

Cook pine nuts in oil until lightly browned. Remove. Cook mushrooms, onion, savory, pepper, and salt to taste until vegetables are tender. Add spinach and cook until spinach wilts and all liquid evaporates. Mix eggs and milk: stir into spinach mixture with cheese. Pour egg mixture into pie crust, sprinkle with pine nuts. Bake at 400° for 25-30 minutes.

JACK OF SPADES COQUILLES

1 pound scallops
3/4 pound sliced mushrooms
4-5 tablespoons margarine
2 tablespoons lemon juice
1 cup dry white wine
1/4 teaspoon thyme
1 bay leaf
3 tablespoons flour
1 cup light cream
buttered bread crumbs
Parmesan cheese
salt and pepper to taste

Sauté mushrooms in margarine, stir in lemon juice and set aside. In pan, combine wine, thyme, bay leaf, salt and pepper, and scallops. Bring to a boil; lower heat and simmer 10 minutes. Drain; reserve 1 cup of broth. Make a sauce of 3 tablespoons margarine, flour, cream and reserved scallop broth. Cook until thickened. Add scallops and mushrooms to sauce. Spoon into 8 scallop shells and top with buttered crumbs and Parmesan cheese. Bake at 400° about 10 minutes. May be made ahead and refrigerated. A special lunch for your bridge club. Add a green salad and bread sticks to complete menu.

CRAB LOUIE

Serves 4

2 cups crabmeat
1/2 cup French dressing
1/3 cup chili sauce
2 tablespoons mayonnaise
1/2 teaspoon Worcestershire sauce
salt and pepper, to taste
2 hard-cooked eggs, sliced
chopped chives
shredded lettuce

Put shredded lettuce on four plates. Top with 1/2 cup crabmeat. Mix other ingredients and pour over crabmeat. Top with 1/2 sliced egg per plate and then chopped chives.

REDOUBLE CRAB SALAD

Serves 12

2 boxes lemon jello
2 cups hot water
1 tablespoon grated onion

1 cup mayonnaise
1 cup whipped cream
3 chopped hard-boiled eggs
1/3 pound Cheddar cheese, diced
2 tablespoons green pepper
1 cup celery
1 cup almonds
2 cups crabmeat
1 1/2 tablespoons olive juice

Mix and chill until thickened. Add rest of ingredients and chill until set.

NANCY'S SEAFOOD QUESADILLA

Serves 4

1 onion, sliced
1 red pepper, sliced
1/4 pound mushrooms, sliced
1 pound whitefish, cubed
1/2 pound crab, shrimp or squid
1 1/2 cups grated Cheddar cheese
1 cup sour cream
1/2 teaspoon basil
1/2 teaspoon oregano
2 cloves garlic
1/2 cup white wine
4 flour tortillas
salt and pepper, to taste

Sauté onions, pepper and mushrooms. Add garlic, basil, oregano; cook 1 minute. Add wine and bring to a boil. Top with seafood; cover pan and simmer 2-3 minutes or until fish flakes. Add salt and pepper to taste. Spoon mixture on large warmed flour tortilla and top with cheese and sour cream. Roll up and serve with salsa.

FIRST BID CRAB

Serves 10

1 cup bread crumbs
1/2 cup milk
1 cup sour cream
1 tablespoon minced onion
1/4 teaspoon mustard
6 drops of Tabasco sauce
1/2 cup olive oil
1/4 pound fresh mushrooms, sliced
2 cups crabmeat
2 teaspoons margarine

Butter 10 ramkins or seafood shells. Soak crumbs in milk and add other ingredients except crabmeat and blend. Fold in crabmeat and divide among dishes. Refrigerate, covered, overnight. Sprinkle with crumbs and dot with margarine. Bake 15 minutes at 400°.

AZTEC PIE

Serves 6-8

1/4 cup vegetable oil
8 corn tortillas
1 8-ounce can tomato sauce
1 cup dairy sour cream
3 cooked chicken breasts, skinned,
  boned and sliced
1/2 cup medium pitted black olives,
  sliced
1/2 cup fresh mushrooms, sliced
1/2 cup jalapeno peppers
3/4 cup grated Monterey Jack cheese
1/2 to 1 cup chicken stock

Heat vegetable oil and fry tortillas individually until each is soft. Combine tomato sauce, sour cream and cook for 5 minutes. Grease a 9″ ovenproof plate. Add a layer of sauce, a tortilla, a layer of chicken, olives, mushrooms, peppers and cheese. Dip the next tortilla in the sauce and make another layer of all the ingredients, and continue until all the ingredients are used. Finish with a layer of tortilla, some olives, mushrooms and jalapenos. Add the chicken stock and sprinkle with cheese. Bake at 350″ for 15-20 minutes.

QUESADILLA

Single Serving

Fry one 12″ flour tortilla in a little olive oil until brown and puffed. Add fillings: one, two or all.

grated sharp Cheddar cheese *or*
diced green chilies *or*
sliced green onions or chives *or*
leftover meat — steak, pork, lamb or chicken *or*
avocado

Put another tortilla on top and flip over. Fry until browned and fillings are hot and cheese is melted. Serve with salsa, sour cream, etc.

STRATA OLÉ

6 flour tortillas, cut in half
2 tablespoons margarine
1 cup chopped onion
1 clove minced garlic
1 teaspoon oregano leaves
1/2 teaspoon ground cumin
1 16-ounce can refried beans
1/2 sliced ripe olives
1 7-ounce can chopped green chilies
2 cups shredded Cheddar cheese
4 eggs
2 cups milk

Arrange half tortillas, overlapping in greased 13″ x 9″ baking dish. Cook onion, garlic, oregano, and cumin in margarine for 2-3 minutes. Heat beans; stir in olives and chilies. Spoon half of the mixture over tortillas and sprinkle with half the cheese. Repeat layers. Beat eggs and milk together and pour over casserole. Bake at 350° for 40 minutes until puffed and golden. Let stand 10 minutes before serving. Serve with salsa, guacamole and sour cream.

B.B. PESTO

2 cups fresh basil leaves, washed and
  dried
4 large garlic cloves, peeled
1 1/2 cups pine nuts (or walnuts)
1 cup good quality olive oil
1 cup freshly grated Parmesan cheese

Everyone has their favorite pesto recipe. I start with these basics and then taste to refine it. Pesto freezes well — the nuts can be added before or after freezing, as you prefer. Blend the basil leaves, garlic, cloves and nuts in cusinart; then add the olive oil with the machine running. Turn off and add the cheese, blending briefly. When freezing for a long period float a little olive oil on top to be mixed in when ready to use.

ACES

MAIN COURSES

HOPPIE'S GINGER PORK

Serves 4-6

2 pounds lean pork in 2″ cubes
1/4 cup oil
1 cup finely chopped onion
2 cloves minced garlic
1/2 cup soy sauce
1 tablespoon finely chopped ginger
2 tablespoons rice vinegar
1 tablespoon sesame seeds

Sauté pork on all sides until brown, at least 20 minutes. Add onions, garlic, and cook 10 minutes. Stir in soy sauce, ginger, and vinegar; simmer 20 minutes. When ready to serve, sprinkle sesame seeds over pork. Serve with rice for a main dish or sliced for dipping in hot mustard for hors d' oeuvres.

PROVENCE LAMB STEW

Serves 6-8

1 1/2 pounds lamb stew meat
1 large onion cut up
1 can whole tomatoes and juice
1 cup white wine
2 tablespoons cognac
Herbs de Provence
garlic

Brown onion in margarine. Flour meat and brown in additional margarine; add tomatoes and put all in casserole. Add 1 cup of wine and garlic; cook, scraping up all loose particles. Add herbs to lamb and also to wine mixture. Pour into casserole. Heat a little cognac and flame and add to the casserole for a special taste.

SAGE LAMB CHOPS

Serves 2

4 lamb chops
2 tablespoons chopped fresh sage
freshly ground pepper
2 tablespoons green onions, chopped
1 cup red wine
2 small bay leaves
1/4 teaspoon thyme
1/4 cup sliced Calamato olives

Sprinkle both sides of lamb chops with sage and pepper; let stand a couple of hours. Broil to desired degree of doneness and serve with sauce made from the remaining ingredients. Brown onions in a little olive oil; add wine and the rest of the ingredients; boil until the sauce is reduced by half. Add the olives and serve on top of the lamb chops.

KINGS PEPPER MARINATED LAMB

Serves 8-10

1/2 cup olive oil
1/2 cup red wine
1/2 cup soy sauce
3 large garlic cloves
3 bay leaves
1 6-pound boned leg of lamb
3 tablespoons whole peppercorns
1 tablespoon unsalted butter

Combine first 5 ingredients and marinate lamb for 24 hours. Bring to room temperature. Remove lamb from marinade. Combine peppercorns and butter and coat lamb. Cook 15 minutes at 450° and then reduce temperature to 350° until thermometer reaches 130°F. in thickest part for medium rare — 45-60 minutes. Let stand 20 minutes before slicing.

LAMB BRIDGE CURRY

Serves 10

3 onions, finely chopped
1/4 pound butter
1 tablespoon cumin
24 cardamon seeds
1 tablespoon coriander
1 1/2 teaspoons pepper
1 1/2 teaspoons ground cloves
1 teaspoon cinnamon
1/4 teaspoon nutmeg
2 teaspoons tumeric
2 tablespoons salt
4 ripe tomatoes, chopped
5 pounds boneless lamb, cut in 1"
  cubes

Sauté onions in butter with seasonings for about 10 minutes. Add lamb; mix and cook over medium heat until it has turned color — about 10 minutes. Stir in tomatoes, cover and simmer 1 1/2 hours. Before serving, reheat in 200° oven about 30 minutes. Serve with rice, onions, chilies, chutney, cashews and coconut.

RICE FOR LAMB CURRY

Serves 6

Add 3 cups cold water to 3 cups long grain rice. Stir in 3 teaspoons salt and 2 teaspoons lemon juice. Bring to boil; cover and simmer 15 minutes. Remove from heat and let stand, covered, 15 minutes longer.

ROLLED ROUND STEAK

Serves 6-8

2 round steaks, about 3″ x 5″
turkey slices
ham slices
cheese slices
olive oil
oregano
salt and pepper, to taste
4 hard-boiled eggs
tomato sauce

Put round steaks together after flattening a little. Layer with turkey, ham and cheese. Put olive oil, oregano, salt and pepper on each layer. Put hard-boiled eggs in center and roll up like jelly roll and tie. Cover with tomato sauce and cook at 350° for 20 to 30 minutes. Cut crosswise. Serve with the sauce.

BALANCED HAND ROUND STEAK

Serves 8

3 pounds round steak
1/4 pound sliced mushrooms
1 onion, thinly sliced
1 can pimiento
1 cup bread crumbs
6 stuffed olives
1/2 cup melted butter
1 teaspoon boiling water
1 egg

Pound steaks until thin. Overlap steaks on cutting board and season with salt, pepper, and paprika. Spread with mushrooms and a layer of thinly sliced onions and pimientos. Cover with bread crumbs. Combine butter, water and egg. Drizzle over bread crumbs. Arrange olives in a row on long side of steak and roll meat around olives. Tie roll, flour outside and brown in butter. Roast at 350° for 2 hours with 6 mushrooms, 3 small onions, and 1 cup red wine in the pan. Serve hot or cold.

FLANK STEAK MARINADE

1/4 cup soy sauce
2 tablespoons honey
2 tablespoons vinegar
1 teaspoon garlic salt
1 teaspoon ground ginger
3/4 cup salad oil
1 green onion

Combine all ingredients and marinate flank steak several hours. Broil or cook outside on grill to desired doneness.

JUMP SHIFT BEEF AND LOBSTER

3-4 pounds whole beef tenderloin
1 4-6 ounce lobster tail
1 tablespoon melted margarine
1 1/2 teaspoons lemon juice
7 slices bacon, partially cooked
1 cup chopped green onion
1/4 teaspoon garlic salt
1 cup butter
1 cup dry white wine

Serves 8-12

Cut beef tenderloin lengthwise to within 1/2" of end and spread flat to butterfly. Place lobster tail in boiling water to cover; return to boiling and reduce heat and cook for 5-6 minutes. Remove lobster from shell and cut in half lengthwise and place halves end to end on beef. Combine the melted butter and lemon juice and drizzle on lobster. Close meat around lobster and tie roast together with string. Place on rack in shallow roasting pan and roast 40 minutes for rare. Lay bacon slices on top of roast and cook 5 more minutes. In saucepan, cook green onion in the remaining butter over low heat until tender. Stir in wine and garlic salt and heat. To serve, slice roast and spoon wine sauce over it.

THE KING OF HEARTS TENDERLOIN

Serves 6-8

3-4 pounds whole tenderloin
garlic salt
2-3 strips bacon

Bake at 450° for 30-35 minutes for rare.

DR. A'S MOROCCAN PIE

Serves 6

2 cups chicken, boiled and cut in
** pieces**
2/3 cup figs, cut in small pieces
1/2 pound mushrooms, sliced
1 cup chopped onions
2 teaspoons cinnamon
1/2 teaspoon cardamom

Boil chicken with carrots, onions, celery, cloves, bay leaf, and thyme. Cook 20-30 minutes and save broth. Cook onion and mushrooms until clear and add seasonings and chicken. Make a white sauce using the chicken broth. Lightly brown a frozen pie shell at 400°. Put mixture in pie shell, put on pie top and bake 30 minutes at 350° until brown on top. Sprinkle powdered sugar and cinnamon over pie before serving.

CHICKEN SOPA

Serves 6-8

1 dozen corn tortillas
1/2 pound grated Cheddar cheese
1 cup diced green chilies
1 or 2 jars boned chicken or turkey
1 can cream of mushroom soup
1 can cream of chicken soup
1/4 cup chopped onion
cumin to taste

Fry tortillas to soften and cut in quarters. Mix soups, chilies, cumin and onion together. Layer in casserole the tortillas, chicken, soup mix, and cheese, ending with tortillas and cheese. Bake 30 minutes at 350°. Ten minutes before serving spread sour cream on top. Pass extra sour cream and green salsa sauce.

KING RANCH CHICKEN

Serves 8

1 dozen corn tortillas
chicken stock
1 large hen, stewed, boned, cut in
  bite-sized pieces
1 large chopped green pepper
1 large chopped onion
2-4 tablespoons cooking oil
1 pound shredded Cheddar cheese
1 teaspoon chili powder
garlic powder or salt
1 can condensed cream of chicken
  soup
1 can condensed cream of mushroom
  soup
1 10-ounce can of tomatoes with
  green chilies

Soak tortillas in boiling chicken stock — place in bottom of 3-quart casserole and top with chicken pieces. Sauté green pepper and onion in oil until tender and layer over chicken. Add cheese to casserole and sprinkle with chili powder, garlic powder, and salt. Mix soups and spoon over casserole. Top with canned tomatoes and chilies mix. Bake at 375° for 45 minutes. Freezes well — either before or after baking. Good dish for evening bridge parties.

MANGO CHICKEN

Serves 4

one box of Rice-A-Roni, cooked
1/2 cup orange-mango juice
1 cup raisins
1 cup peanuts
1 cup water chestnuts
1 chicken cooked, and taken off bone
1 mango
chutney
lemon pepper
cooked onions
ginger, chili powder, garlic, soy sauce
** to taste**

Blend all together and top with slivered almonds.

CHICKEN CASHEW

2 cans chicken broth
2 cloves minced garlic
4 whole boned and skinned chicken
  breasts
1 cup sliced carrots
1 cup sliced celery
1 cup broccoli flowerettes
1 cup thinly sliced red onion
1/2 cup peas
2 1/2 tablespoons cornstarch
1 tablespoon water
3/4 cup sour cream
salt and pepper to taste
handful chopped parsley

Topping:
3 cups all purpose flour
1 teaspoon salt
3/4 cup shortening
1 cup chopped cashews
1 cup milk
1 1/2 tablespoons baking powder

Cook chicken pieces in broth with garlic for 15 minutes. Transfer chicken to large serving dish. Add carrots, celery, broccoli, onions and peas; bring to a boil and cook 3 minutes. Remove vegetables to casserole. In small bowl mix cornstarch and water; whisk into chicken broth and boil one minute. Remove from heat and add sour cream. Add broth to casserole with parsley, salt and pepper to taste.

In large bowl, sift flour, baking powder, and salt. Cut in shortening until mixture looks like crumbs. Stir in cashews, add milk and mix until it is moist. On floured board, knead 8 times and roll into "cover" for the casserole and bake 20-30 minutes or until chicken is tender.

BENGAL CURRY

Serves 10-12

6 pounds of chicken pieces
1/4 cup margarine
1 large onion
1/4 cup sliced crystalized ginger
dash of mint, pepper, salt, cloves
3 tablespoons curry, or to taste
1 quart milk
3 1/2 ounces flaked coconut
juice of 4 limes
2 cups cream

Brown chicken in margarine until golden. Add chopped onion and cook until limp. Add seasonings; pour in milk and cook slowly 1 1/2 hours until chicken is tender. Stir in coconut, lime juice and cream. Cook until heated through. Serve with rice. Can be made early in day or day before. Suggested condiments: bananas, chutney, chopped peanuts, apple cubes, bacon and raisins.

CHICKEN BREASTS IN SPADES

Serves 6

6 chicken breasts
24 Cheddar cheese crackers
1 cup cottage cheese
1 cup plain yogurt
1 package Lipton's onion soup mix

Blend ingredients and spread on top of the chicken breasts. Splash with dry vermouth and cover with additional crushed Cheddar cheese crackers and paprika. Bake at 300° for 1 1/2 hours.

ONE HEART CHICKEN

Serves 6

6 medium chicken breast halves
1 cup cream of mushroom soup
1 cup chicken soup
1 3-ounce can mushrooms
1 cup sour cream

Combine soups and mushroom liquid and pour over chicken. Sprinkle with Parmesan cheese, paprika and seasoning salt. Bake at 350° for 1 to 1 1/2 hours until tender.

A Microwave Chicken Casserole

BALANCED HAND

Serves 4-6

2 pounds chicken breasts, skinned
  and browned
1 package Knorr mushroom sauce
  mix
1 can chicken broth
1 cup rice (any kind), cooked
basil bread crumbs
slivered almonds

Make soup with Knorr sauce mix and canned chicken broth. Put cooked rice in greased casserole dish, place chicken on top, pour soup mixture over all. Place bread crumbs and slivered almonds on top. Microwave 15 minutes. Basil bread crumbs are made by blending in cuisinart leftover bread and fresh basil.

GARLIC CHICKEN

Serves 2-4

1 broiler chicken halved
1 whole head of garlic
1/2 cup soy sauce
1/2 cup balsamic vinegar
2 tablespoons Worcestershire sauce
1 large tablespoon of mustard

Combine ingredients, rub into chicken and roast at 450° for 15 minutes. Reduce heat to 350° and cook 25 minutes or until tender.

SOUTH OF THE BORDER MEATLOAF

Serves 4

1 pound hamburger
1 cup salsa
1 tablespoon hot taco sauce
1 4-ounce can chopped chilies
1/3 cup of cheese

Blend all ingredients. Bake at 350° for 35-45 minutes. Can put additional cheese on top the last 5 minutes. Serve with salsa.

ENCHILADA CHEESE STACK

1 pound ground beef
1/2 cup vegetable oil
1/2 cup chopped green pepper
1/2 cup chopped red pepper
1 medium onion, chopped
1 large garlic clove, minced
8 ounces salsa
1 teaspoon chili powder
1/4 teaspoon ground cumin
1/3 cup sour cream
1 16-ounce can refried beans
1 medium tomato, chopped
6 flour tortillas
3 cups sharp Cheddar cheese, shredded
sliced ripe olives

Brown beef in half of the oil; add peppers (optional), onion, garlic, chili powder and cumin. Cook until peppers are tender and drain. Add salsa and simmer 5 minutes. Blend in sour cream and remove from heat and keep warm. Heat refried beans with tomatoes and chilies in another skillet and keep warm. Heat remaining oil, fry tortillas quickly until golden and blistered. Drain on paper towels. Place 1 tortilla on baking sheet — top with 1/5 bean mixture, meat mixture and cheese. Be sure to spread to the edge of tortilla. Repeat with remaining 4 tortillas — one on top of another. Top with remaining tortilla. Bake at 375° for 15 minutes. Sprinkle with additional cheese, and bake until cheese is melted. Garnish with olives. Can serve with additional salsa, guacamole, or sour cream. Leftovers can be reheated in microwave.

TEX-MEX CHOPS

6 boneless pork loin chops
1 1/2 tablespoons cooking oil
2 cups chunky salsa
3/4 teaspoon cumin
1 1/2 cups chilies, diced
1/2 cup grated Cheddar cheese

Brown chops quickly. Add salsa, chilies and cumin to the skillet. Lower heat, simmer for 10 minutes, uncover and top each chop with 1 1/2 tablespoons of cheese. Cover and simmer an additional minute or until cheese melts.

JAMBALAYA

3/4 pound country sausage
2 ounces pepperoni, sliced
3/4 cup coarsley chopped green
  pepper
1/2 cup coarsley chopped onion
2 1/2 cups water
1 1/2 cups shrimp, peeled
1 medium tomato, chopped
2 chicken bouillon cubes
1 1/2 cups uncooked white rice
1 tablespoon Worcestershire sauce
1/8 teaspoon garlic powder
1/2 teaspoon thyme
pepper and salt

Cook sausage, pepperoni, green pepper and onion until vegetables are slightly tender. Add water, shrimp, tomato, bouillon cubes and bring to a boil. Stir in rice and seasonings. Cover and cook 30 minutes until rice is tender and liquid is absorbed.

CHEESE STUFFED CALAMARI

8 whole small squid (save tentacles)
1 pound ricotta cheese
1/2 cup grated mozzarella
1/4 cup fresh basil, chopped
1 egg
2 1/2 ounces minced prosciutto
1/2 cup grated parmesan

Marinara Sauce:
4 tablespoons olive oil
1/2 stalk celery, sliced
1 small onion, chopped
2 cloves garlic
2 tablespoons Italian seasoning
1 can chopped tomato
1 cup red wine

Combine stuffing mixture and fill calamari.

Sauté celery and onion in olive oil. Add garlic and seasonings, cook another minute. Add tomatoes, wine and tentacles and simmer 10 minutes. Cover bottom of oiled casserole dish lightly with sauce; place squid on top and cover with remaining sauce. Cover and bake at 350° for 20 minutes. Remove cover and sprinkle with Parmesan cheese and brown.

JANE'S SOLE PIQUANT

Serves 4

1 cup dry white wine
1 tablespoon salt
4 sole filets
1/4 cup green onions chopped
French bread crumbs
1/2 cup mayonnaise
1/2 cup sour cream or yogurt
paprika

Marinate filets in wine and salt for 2 hours. Drain and dry fish. Dip both sides in crumbs and arrange in greased shallow casserole. Combine mayonnaise, sour cream, and green onions. Spread over fish. Cover with thin layers of crumbs and sprinkle with paprika. Bake at 400° for 15 minutes until it flakes with fork.

ORANGE ROUGHIE

Serves 4

1/2 cube margarine
4 orange roughie filets
mayonnaise
1 packet of Good Season Garlic
  Dressing
lemon juice or white wine

Dip fish in melted margarine and lay in pan. Spread with mayonnaise and contents of Good Season Garlic Dressing mix. Sprinkle this with lemon juice or white wine. Cover with bread crumbs and Parmesan cheese, if desired. Bake 15 minutes at 400°.

MICROWAVE SOLE

Cover each sole filet with salt and pepper to taste and thin slices of lemon. Wrap each in lettuce leaf and cook on high 3 minutes on each side. Can use any fish, but thicker filets would take longer. As fish swells the lettuce leaf keeps the fish moist.

NORTH OF THE BORDER CHICKEN

Serves 10-12

6 pounds chicken
3/4 cup flour
2 teaspoons salt
1/2 teaspoon pepper
1 1/2 teaspoons paprika
1/4 cup margarine
1/4 cup shortening
1 cup slivered almonds, browned
1 1/4 cups water
1 can chicken consomme
2 teaspoons catsup
1 cup sour cream
1 14-ounce can of peach halves,
  drained
1 cup chutney

Brown chicken after dusting with flour, salt, pepper and paprika in margarine and shortening. Place in baking dish. Stir remaining seasonings (from chicken dusting) with water, chicken consomme, and castup; cook until thick. Stir in sour cream and pour over the chicken. Cover and bake at 350° for 1 hour. Place peach halves on top with chutney in the cavities and cook uncovered for 20 minutes more.

FAJITAS

Serving size depends on size of flank steak.

flank steak
flour tortillas
sour cream
guacamole
salsa
onion (optional)
green pepper (optional)
1/4 cup olive oil
2 tablespoons lime juice
1 clove garlic

Marinate flank steak in oil, lime juice and garlic. Cook on outside grill or broil to desired doneness. If desired, slice and cook onion and green pepper to put in with meat strips in flour tortillas that have been warmed. Serve with sour cream, guacamole and salsa. To warm tortillas — place in damp cloth, heat in 300° oven 10-15 minutes. In microwave, place between paper towels and heat on high 1-2 minutes.

FOURTH OF JULY DOGS

Serves 8

2 16-ounce cans of chili with beans
1 7-ounce can of diced green chilies
1/4 cup chopped green onions
8 hot dogs and buns
1 cup chunky hot salsa
1 cup Cheddar cheese, shredded

Mix together and heat the beans, chilies and green onions. Cook over medium heat for 10 minutes stirring frequently. Grill hot dogs and put in heated buns. Top with chili mixture, salsa and shredded cheese.

GINA'S SPAGHETTI

Serves 4-6

1 big onion, chopped
2 cloves minced garlic
1 green pepper chopped
1 pound ground round
a little parsley
1 #2 can tomatoes
2 small cans tomato paste
2 bay leaves
pinch of oregano
pinch of rosemary
1 can of mushrooms, including juice
salt and pepper to taste

Brown onion, garlic and green pepper in oil; add the meat and parsley. Cook until done, then add tomatoes, tomato paste, bay leaves, oregano, rosemary, mushrooms, salt and pepper. Simmer several hours and add water if it becomes too thick. This freezes wonderfuly. A Kansas friend gave this to me before I was married and our family has been using it ever since.

NO BID PAELLA

1/8 teaspoon saffron
1/4 cup olive oil
1 onion chopped
1 red pepper chopped
2 cloves minced garlic
2 ripe tomatoes, peeled and chopped
4 cups hot chicken stock
2 cups long-grain rice uncooked
2 chorizo sausages, cut in 1/2-inch
  slices
8-10 chicken drumsticks
12 large shrimp
12 mussels or littleneck clams
salt, pepper, cayenne pepper to taste

Heat the olive oil and sauté the onions, pepper and garlic over medium heat for 3 minutes. Add the tomatoes and cook over high heat for 2 minutes. Stir in the rice and cook for 1 minute until lightly browned. Meanwhile, lightly brown the sausage in olive oil. Discard all but 2 tablespoons fat and brown the drumsticks on all sides. Peel and devein the shrimp and scrub the mussels or clams. Add the hot chicken stock in which the saffron has been dissolved to the rice mixture and loosely cover the pan and bake for 15 minutes at 400°. Add the shrimp and mussels and continue baking for another 10-15 minutes or until the rice is cooked. If there's too much liquid uncover the pan the last 15 minutes of baking. Correct the seasoning and serve the paella in the pan in which it was cooked. Serve with a salad and pita bread for your couples bridge club.

FINESSE

VEGETABLES & SIDE DISHES

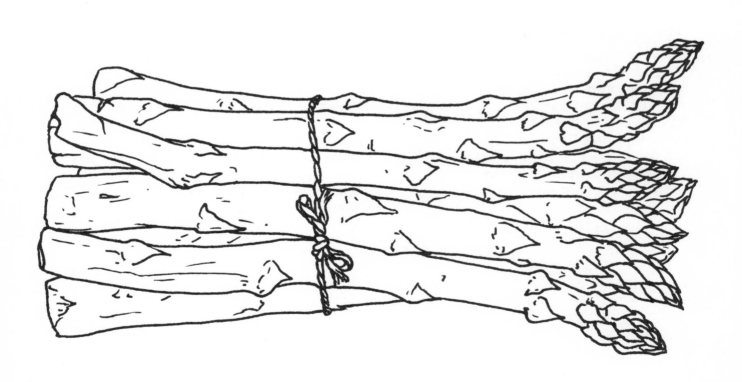

EGGPLANT

Serves 6

1 eggplant, skinned and chopped
1 cup chopped onion, sautéed
1 cup basil bread crumbs
Cheddar cheese

Simmer eggplant until tender. Put eggplant in baking dish. Top with sautéed onions, Cheddar cheese and basil bread crumbs. Bake at 375° to 30 minutes.

BAB'S MUSHROOMS

Serves 2-4

1 onion, chopped
1/2 pound mushrooms, sliced
3 tablespoons sour cream
2 tablespoons flour
1/2 can chicken broth
2 tablespoons Parmesan cheese
salt to taste
1 tablespoon minced green onion
1 tablespoon parsley

Brown onion quickly over high heat; add mushrooms and continue cooking and stirring over high heat until liquid has boiled off. Sprinkle with flour; add broth and cook until thick. Add green onion, parsley, sour cream and Parmesan cheese. Cover with basil bread crumbs just before serving and reheat if necessary in microwave. Can be used as a side dish or over toast points for brunch.

CREAMED MUSHROOMS

Serves 6-8

2 pounds fresh mushrooms
4 tablespoons margarine
4 tablespoons dry sherry
2 cups sour cream
1 package Good Seasoning cheese-
   garlic mix
salt and pepper to taste

Sauté sliced mushrooms in margarine until liquid is gone. Add sherry and other ingredients. Cook over low heat until thickened — add more sherry if too thick. Good with beef, or over toast for brunch.

BLANCHE'S ASPARAGUS

Serves 4-6

1 package frozen or 1 bunch fresh
   asparagus
1 cup mushroom soup
1/2 cup shredded almonds
buttered crumbs

Cook asparagus 3 minutes. Arrange asparagus and soup in alternate layers, and sprinkle with almonds. Final layer is soup sprinkled with buttered crumbs. Bake 25-30 minutes in 350° oven. A really old family recipe!

ASPARAGUS PARMESAN

Serves 2-4

1 pound asparagus, cooked, rinsed
  with cold water, and drained
1/4 pound margarine, melted
3 tablespoons lemon juice
1/2 cup grated Parmesan cheese,
  fresh
bread crumbs (with basil and
  cayenne, optional)
paprika
chopped almonds

Place cooked asparagus spears in casserole dish. Mix margarine and lemon juice and pour over spears. Top with Parmesan cheese, paprika, bread crumbs and chopped almonds. Place in hot oven 425° for 15 minutes.

ASPARAGUS CASSEROLE

Serves 4

2 pounds asparagus, slightly cooked
2 cans golden mushroom soup
1 pound grated Cheddar cheese

Put asparagus in rectangular casserole. Stir soup and pour over asparagus. Cover with grated cheese. Bake at 350° for 30-40 minutes.

HEARTS OF SPINACH-MUSHROOM CASSEROLE

Serves 6-8

2 packages frozen chopped spinach
1 8-ounce can tomato sauce
1 cup cooked sliced mushrooms
1/3 cup grated Parmesan cheese
1 cup sour cream

Cook spinach; drain well. Add tomato sauce, mushrooms, and sour cream. Top with Parmesan cheese and bake in covered casserole 30 minutes at 325°.

SPINACH SOUFFLE

Serves 2

**1 package of frozen chopped spinach,
  defrosted and drained**
1/2 cup sour cream
1 package onion soup mix

Mix all together and place in a buttered casserole. Sprinkle with seasoned bread crumbs. Bake at 350° for 20 minutes.

What's Trump?

BAKED APPLES WITH MINCEMEAT

Serves 8

8 large apples, cored
3/4 cup mincemeat
3/4 cup currant jelly, melted

Place apples in casserole and add water to cover 1/4 of apples. Stuff with mincemeat. Pour melted jelly over each apple and bake at 350° until apples are tender to the fork — about 45 minutes. Baste from time to time. Serve hot or cold. Wonderful with poultry. For dessert, add whipped cream.

ACORN SQUASH

Serves 4

2 acorn squash
lemon juice
1/4 cup raisins
1 1/2 cups applesauce
1/4 cup brown sugar

Halve and seed squash. Mix rest of ingredients together and fill the squash. Cover and bake 1 hour until tender.

SIDE SUIT TOMATOES   *One tomato per serving*

Broil tomatoes at 425° for 5-8 minutes until just tender, but not mushy and cover with:

1/2 cup sour cream   Combine and cover tomato with mixture.
1/4 cup mayonnaise
2 tablespoons chopped onion
1/2 teaspoon dill seed
or

butter   Combine and cover tomato with mixture.
Parmesan cheese
salt and pepper
or

1/4 cup onion   Combine and cover tomato with mixture.
2 tablespoons bread crumbs
1/4 cup parsley
1/4 teaspoon basil
1/2 teaspoon minced garlic
2 tablespoons margarine

TOMATOES FOR A BRIDGE PARTY

Serves 8-10

Peel and slice 4 tomatoes, a cucumber and 3 or 4 green onions. Place in shallow dish and sprinkle with fresh basil leaves and parsley. Mix well:

1/4 cup salad oil
1 tablespoon lemon juice
1/2 teaspoon minced garlic
1/2 teaspoon salt
1/2 teaspoon oregano leaves

Pour over tomatoes and chill, covered, 1 hour. Nice dish for a buffet.

QUEEN OF HEARTS TOMATO DISH

Serves 6-8

2 pint boxes cherry tomatoes
1 large onion, chopped
1 green pepper, chopped
1 1/4 teaspoons chili powder
1 1/4 teaspoons oregano
salt and pepper, to taste
1 cup bread crumbs
2 tablespoons margarine
2 cups Cheddar cheese, grated

Spread whole tomatoes in a buttered deep casserole dish evenly. Cover with onions and peppers. Mix spices with the bread crumbs and sprinkle over the vegetables. Dot with margarine and cover with the cheese. Bake uncovered in 375° oven for 30 minutes.

This may set you and your partner!

ZUCCHINI CHILI CASSEROLE

Serves 10-12

2 cups cooked rice
1 7-ounce can whole green chilies, chopped
1 4-ounce can green chili salsa
3 zucchini, diced and blanched
1 tomato, sliced
2 teaspoons chopped onion
2 teaspoons chopped green pepper
1 teaspoon salt
1 teaspoon oregano
1 pound Cheddar cheese, grated
2 cups sour cream

In a greased 10″ casserole, layer rice, chilies, salsa, zucchini, tomato, onion, green pepper, seasonings and cheese. Cover with sour cream. Bake uncovered for 30 minutes at 350°; then at 325° for 40 minutes.

SIX CLUBS ZUCCHINI

Serves 10-12

6 cups sliced zucchini, cooked
2 egg yolks, beaten
1 cup sour cream
2 tablespoons flour
2 beaten egg whites
1 1/2 cups sharp Cheddar cheese
1 tablespoon butter
1/4 cup buttered bread crumbs

Combine egg yolks, sour cream, flour, and fold in beaten egg whites. Layer 1/2 zucchini, 1/2 egg mixture, 1/2 cheese. Repeat layers and cover top with crumbs. Bake 350° for 20-25 minutes.

PLEASE PASS THE CARROTS

Serves 16

5 cups carrots, cooked crisp
1 onion sliced
1 green pepper cut in strips
1 cup sugar
1 cup red wine vinegar with garlic
1 tablespoon prepared mustard
1 teaspoon salt
1 1/2 teaspoons pepper
3 teaspoons garlic salt
1 can tomato soup
1/2 cup vegetable oil
1 tablespoon Worcestershire sauce

Put carrots, onions and green pepper in attractive glass bowl. Mix remaining ingredients separately and pour over vegetables. Marinate in refrigerator 12 hours. This is an oldie with different ingredients — good — and keeps in refrigerator for 2-3 weeks.

BAB'S RICE

Serves 6-8

2 cups uncooked white rice
8-10 large fresh mushrooms, sliced
3-4 green onions, sliced
1 cup sour cream
4-6 ounces sharp Cheddar cheese,
  grated

Cook rice. Sauté mushrooms and onions in margarine. When rice is cooked, add other ingredients. Can be cooked early in day and reheated in microwave or frozen and reheated.

ZUCCHINI-CHEESE SIDE DISH

Serves 10-12

5 zucchini, sliced 1/2" thick
1 large onion, sliced
4-5 large tomatoes, sliced
1/2 cup chopped parsley
1/2 cup fresh basil leaves, chopped
2 cups grated Swiss cheese
salt and pepper, to taste

Layer vegetables and herbs in casserole. Sprinkle with salt and pepper. Cover and bake 45 minutes or microwave on high 12 minutes, or until tender. Remove cover; add cheese and bake 15 minutes, or until cheese is melted. (Microwave 5-6 minutes.)

GLAZED CARROTS WITH FRESH MINT

Serves 8-10

1 bunch carrots
5 tablespoons butter
1 1/2 tablespoons brown sugar
1/4 cup chopped fresh mint

Peel and cut carrots. Steam carrots until just tender. Drain; add butter, brown sugar and mint.

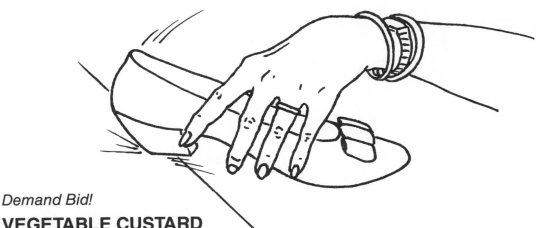

Demand Bid!

VEGETABLE CUSTARD

Serves 6

8 eggs
4 tablespoons margarine
1 pound potatoes, peeled and cut into
** 1/2" cubes**
1 small bunch broccoli, diced
1 green pepper, diced
1 pimiento, diced
1 small onion, diced
1/2 teaspoon salt
1 8-ounce sour cream
1/2 pound sharp Cheddar cheese,
** shredded**

Grease 12" x 8" dish. Separate 6 eggs. Cook potatoes, broccoli, pepper, pimiento, onion, and salt until vegetables are tender in margarine, stirring frequently. Put into casserole. Into egg yolks stir sour cream, 1/3 cup water, and remaining 2 whole eggs. Pour custard mixture over vegetables in casserole. Sprinkle with half of shredded cheese. Beat egg whites until stiff and fold in remaining shredded cheese. Spread meringue over vegetables and bake 35 minutes at 350° until knife inserted into custard comes out clean.

CUCUMBER SIDE DISH

1 cucumber, peeled, scored and
  sliced
3 green onions, sliced
1 1/2 teaspoons Lawry's seasoned
  salt

Let stand for 15-20 minutes, then pour off liquid.

Add:
1/2 cup sour cream
2 teaspoons mayonnaise
1 1/2 tablespoons vinegar
1/4 teaspoon seasoned salt
1 teaspoon dill weed

Marinate overnight.
Can use as a side dish or to make cucumber sandwiches. Spread bread circles with mixture of mayonnaise, horseradish sauce, lemon juice and cayenne. Blot cucumbers on paper towels and put on top of bread circles.

GREEN ONION PIE

Serves 6

3 cups green onions, sliced
1/4 cup margarine
4 eggs, slightly beaten
2 cups light cream, scalded
salt and pepper to taste
1 pie shell, unbaked

Mix together and bake at 350° for 30-40 minutes.

This is forcing to game and fame.

MEXICAN CHEESE "FUDGE"

Serves 6-8

9 ounces Cheddar cheese, grated
9 ounces Monterey Jack cheese,
  shredded
3 eggs
1/2 cup salsa
1 tablespoon flour
1 small can diced green chilies

Combine cheeses and sprinkle half in bottom of 9" x 9" pan. Beat eggs and flour; mix with salsa and chilies and pour over cheese. Sprinkle remaining cheese on top. Bake at 350° for 30 minutes and cool slightly before cutting in squares. Serve it as a dinner accompaniment with additional salsa.

CELERY AU GRATIN

Serves 8

6 cups diced celery
2 cans water chestnuts, well drained
2 cans cream of chicken soup
seasoned oyster crackers
toasted almond slices

Cook celery with 2 tablespoons water in microwave for 2 minutes or until almost tender; drain. Season; add next 2 ingredients. Cover with seasoned oyster crackers or bread crumbs and toasted almond slivers. Heat at 325° for 20 minutes.

DIAMOND CELERY BAKE

Serves 10-12

4 cups thinly sliced celery
4 tablespoons margarine
3 tablespoons flour
1 cup milk
1/2 cup mushrooms, cooked and
  chopped
2 tablespoons green pepper, chopped
2 tablespoons pimiento, chopped
4 ounces Cheddar cheese, grated
1 cup bread crumbs
2 tablespoons margarine
salt to taste

Cook celery in margarine 5 minutes. Remove and set aside in bowl. Stir in flour and salt and add milk, stirring until mixture is thick. Stir in mushrooms, green pepper and pimiento. Add cheese and stir until blended; add celery. Spoon mixture into oiled 1 quart casserole and cover with bread crumbs and additional 2 tablespoons of margarine. Bake uncovered in 350° oven for 20 minutes — celery should be crisp.

FOUR CARD VEGETABLES

Serves 6-8

1 bag (16-ounces) frozen broccoli,
  carrots, and cauliflower combination
1/2 cup sliced cooked mushrooms
1 can cream of mushroom soup
1 cup sharp Cheddar cheese
1/3 cup sour cream
2 cans French fried onions

Combine vegetables, soup, 1/2 of cheese, sour cream and one can of onions. Pour into a 1-quart casserole. Bake covered at 350° for 30 minutes. Top with remaining cheese and second can of onions. Bake uncovered 5 minutes more.

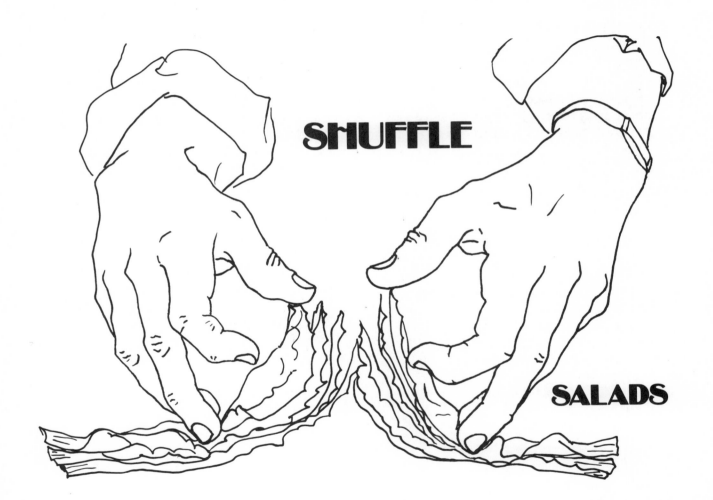

Here's your opening Three Bid.

SUPER DIP OR SALAD

1 1/2 large onions, chopped
1 1/2 pounds ground beef
1 large can refried beans
1 large can diced green chiles
2 cups shredded Cheddar cheese
1 7-ounce bottle prepared taco sauce

Brown onions and ground beef and drain. Add salt and pepper to taste. Used as a dip, casserole, or salad. Layer as follows: refried beens, beef and onion mixture, green chilies, sauce, and cheese.

For dip: Heat at 350° for 15 minutes — add nachos around edge and serve.

For casserole: Bake in 9" x 13" baking dish at 350° for 30 minutes. Can top with green onions and black chopped olives. Serve with avocado and sour cream.

For taco salad: Buy or make tortilla cups and fill with shredded lettuce. Put hot taco mixture on top of lettuce. Serve with olives, onions, sour cream and guacamole.

CHICKEN SALAD WITH MACADAMIAS

Serves 4-6

**Boil 1 chicken until tender, cool and
  remove from bones and cut in
  chunks
1 cup chopped celery
1 cup chopped green onions
salt and pepper to taste
1 cup ground Macadamia nuts
mayonnaise**

Mix with mayonnaise and serve on
lettuce leaf. (Can mix 1 teaspoon curry
powder with mayonnaise if desired.)

HOT CHICKEN SALAD

Serves 6

**2 cups cut up cooked chicken
2 cups cut up celery
1/2 cup sliced almonds
3/4 cup grated Cheddar cheese
2 teaspoons minced onion
2 teaspoons lemon rind
1 cup mayonnaise
1 cup potato chips
salt and pepper, to taste**

Mix all ingredients except potato chips
and put in casserole. Cover with chips.
Bake at 400° for 10 minutes.

HAWAIIAN CHICKEN SALAD

Serves 10-12

1/2 cup long grain white rice
1/2 cup wild rice
3 cups cooked chicken in cubes
1/2 cup raisins
1/2 cup sliced green onion
1 cup salad oil
1/2 cup white-wine vinegar
1 1/2 tablespoons Dijon mustard
2 cloves garlic
1 1/2 teaspoons salt
3/4 teaspoon red hot pepper sauce
3/4 cup Macadamia nuts

Prepare wild and white rice in separate pans at least 4 hours before serving. Cool to room temperature. In large bowl combine rices, chicken, raisins, and green onions. In a small jar combine oil, vinegar, mustard, garlic, salt and red pepper. Stir and pour over rice; cover and refrigerate 2-3 hours. Just before serving, add nuts.

CHICKEN SALAD FOR THE CLUB

Serves 10-12

1 package chicken Rice-A-Roni
6 green onions
1/2 cup green pepper
1/2 cup stuffed green olives
2 6-ounce jars marinated artichoke
  hearts
1/2 teaspoon curry
1/3 cup mayonnaise
3 cups diced chicken

Cook rice according to instructions recipe calls for, omitting butter. Add onion, pepper, artichoke and green olives. Mix artichoke liquid with curry and mayonnaise. Toss with rice, chicken and vegetables and refrigerate 24 hours.

POTATO SALAD

4 cups boiling potatoes
1/2 cup white wine vinegar
1/2 cup olive oil
salt and pepper, to taste
1 cup thinly sliced red onions
1 cup celery, sliced
1 medium cucumber, peeled and
  seeded
2 cups mayonnaise
5 tablespoons Dijon mustard
24 hard-cooked eggs
1 cup parsley

Cook potatotes until tender, but still firm; drain, slice, and sprinkle with vinegar, olive oil, salt and pepper. Add onions, celery, cucumbers, mayonnaise, and mustard. Toss to combine, then add quarted eggs and parsley. Cool to room temperature, cover and refrigerate overnight.

ASPIC OF CUCUMBER

2 tablespoons unflavored gelatin
1/4 cup water
1 cup boiling water
1/3 cup sugar
1/2 cup cider vinegar
1 grated onion
1 cup grated cucumber
lemon juice and salt, to taste

Soak gelatin in water 3-5 minutes. Add boiling water, sugar, salt, vinegar, and lemon juice. When it starts to thicken stir in onion and cucumber.

APPLE RAISIN SALAD

Serves 6

1/2 cup raisins
2 apples diced
1 teaspoon lemon juice
1 cup celery, sliced
1 cup carrot, shredded
1/2 cup walnuts, chopped
1/4 cup sour cream
1/2 cup mayonnaise

Plump raisins in hot water, drain and cool. Toss apples with lemon juice and mix all together. Combine sour cream and mayonnaise and toss.

MANDARIN SALAD

Serves 6-8

Assorted salad greens
2-3 slices bacon, fried crisp and
  crumbled
3-4 green onions, sliced
1 cup mandarin oranges, drained

Dressing:
2 tablespoons vinegar
1/4 teaspoon dried tarragon
1/4 teaspoon pepper
1/2 teaspoon dried basil
1/2 teaspoon salt
1/4 cup olive oil

Combine dressing ingredients in glass jar and shake well. Toss with greens and other ingredients. Use enough greens for 6-8 servings.

BOUILLABAISSE SALAD

1/2 pound crabmeat
1/2 pound cooked lobster, chopped
1/2 pound shrimp, cooked, peeled, deveined
1 cup lemon juice
1 head leaf lettuce
1 head Romaine lettuce
1 pint cherry tomatoes, cut in half
8 ripe olives, cut in half
1 bunch watercress
salt and pepper, to taste

Mix fish, lemon juice, salt and pepper and toss. Chill. Place leaf lettuce and Romaine on platter. Top with seafood and garnish with tomatoes, olives and watercress. Serve with your favorite dressing.

SEGO LILY SALAD

1 head Romaine lettuce
1 head red leaf lettuce
1/2 pound spinach
2 cups mandarin oranges, drained
1 1/2 cups crumbled feta cheese
1/2 pound bacon, cooked and
  crumbled
1/2 medium red onion, sliced in rings
1 avocado, cut in chunks

Combine lettuce, spinach leaves,
orange segments, cheese, bacon and
red onion slices.

Dressing:
1/4 cup sugar
1 teaspoon grated onion
1 teaspoon dry mustard
1 teaspoon salt
1/3 cup cider vinegar
1 cup oil
1 teaspoon poppy seeds
1 teaspoon sesame seeds

Combine sugar, grated onion, mustard,
salt and vinegar and blend with a whisk.
Add oil gradually, blending well. Stir in
poppy seeds and sesame seeds and
toss salad with dressing.

HEART AND CLUB SALAD

Serves 10-12

4 medium tomatoes
1 large salad onion
2 cans large pitted ripe olives, sliced
2 1/2 pounds fresh mushrooms, sliced
1 package Good Season Italian
  dressing mix

Layer vegetables and sprinkle Good Season dressing on each layer. Pour one bottle of your favorite Italian dressing over all and let stand for an hour, then chill before serving.

LAYER SALAD

Serves 8-10

2 bunches shredded raw spinach
salt, pepper and sugar
1 pound bacon, crumbled
6 sliced hard-boiled eggs
1 can sliced water chestnuts
salt, pepper and sugar
10 ounce package frozen peas
1/2 sliced red onion

Dressing:
1 cup Swiss cheese, grated
1 cup mayonnaise
1 cup Miracle Whip dressing
1 package Good Season Italian
  dressing

Layer as listed. Combine 1 cup mayonnaise, 1 cup Miracle Whip, 1 package Good Seasons Italian dressing (dry). Spread on top. Grate Swiss cheese over all. Refrigerate at least 12 hours.

Dieting foursome?

CUCUMBER, TOMATO AND ONION

Serves 8-10

1 cucumber, peeled, seeded and
  chopped
3 tomatoes, seeded and chopped
1 large onion, thinly sliced
3 cloves garlic, finely chopped
1/4 cup chopped parsley
1/4 cup lemon juice
1 seeded chopped chili pepper
salt and pepper, to taste

Mix, chill, serve!!!

TOMATO PIMIENTO

Serves 1

Thick slice beefsteak tomato. Cover with whole pimiento, top with anchovy. Italian
dressing to taste.

LUNCH BRUNCH SALAD

Serves 4

1 bunch watercress, remove stems
1 papaya, cut in slices
1 cup broken pecans
spicy French dressing, to taste

Mix.

ASPARAGUS-LEEK SALAD

Serves 4

1 pound fresh asparagus
1 cup thinly sliced leeks or green
  onions
1/2 cup halved cherry tomatoes
1/3 cup salad oil
2 tablespoons lemon juice
1/2 teaspoon dried tarragon, crushed
1/8 teaspoon salt and pepper

Cook asparagus in boiling salted water 5 minutes. Drain and transfer asparagus to dish. Cool to room temperature and sprinkle with leeks and cherry tomatoes. Combine other ingredients in jar, cover, and shake well. Pour over asparagus and chill. Serve on lettuce leaf.

SPINACH SALAD

Serves 4

1 pound fresh spinach
4 cups cooked chicken or 1 1/2
  pounds ham cut into strips
1 cucumber, sliced
1/4 pound fresh mushrooms, sliced
2 tomatoes, sliced

Wash and tear spinach into bite-sized pieces. Arrange spinach, chicken (or ham), tomatoes, mushrooms, and cucumber on luncheon plates and serve with avocado dressing.

Avocado Dressing:
2 ripe avocados
4 tablespoons lemon juice
1 cup sour cream or yogurt
2 teaspoons minced onions

Cut one avocado into 1/2″ chunks and toss with 2 tablespoons lemon juice. In blender, process remaining dressing ingredients until smooth. Stir in avocado and serve on spinach salad. Good dressing for just spinach, tomato and mushrooms.

RED CLOVER SALAD

Serves 10

1/2 pound spinach, finely chopped
1/2 cup celery, finely chopped
1/2 cup onion, finely chopped
1 cup Old English cheese, in small
  cubes
4 hard-cooked eggs, chopped

Toss ingredients and add dressing.

Dressing:
1 1/4 cups mayonnaise
1/2 teaspoon Tabasco sauce
1 1/2 teaspoons vinegar
1/4 teaspoon horseradish
salt to taste

Mix dressing. Garnish salad with grated whole egg.

GLORIA'S FRUIT SALAD

Serves 10-12

2 cups peach slices
2 cups blueberries
2 cups strawberries
2 cups grapes
2 tablespoons chopped nuts

Layer sliced fruit in a large straight-sided glass bowl. Mix the dressing ingredients and put on top of the layer fruit and chill in the refrigerator.

Dressing:
8 ounces cream cheese, softened
1 teaspoon grated lemon rind
1/2 cup whipping cream
1/4 cup powdered sugar

KIWI FRUIT SALAD

Combine chunks of watermelon, slices of banana, fresh peaches, strawberries and kiwi. Use strawberry yogurt with a little lemon juice added for the dressing.

MARINADE FOR MUSHROOMS

Serves 4-6

juice of one lemon
1 lemon, cut into thin rounds
3/4 cup oil
1/4 cup red wine vinegar
2 cloves garlic
1/4 teaspoon pepper
1/2 teaspoon salt
fresh parsley for garnish
1 pound mushrooms, sliced

Clean mushrooms, place in saucepan and toss with lemon juice. Add oil, vinegar, garlic, pepper and salt; cook and stir over medium high heat 5 minutes. Cool to room temperature, chill. Cover a serving plate with fresh parsley, top with lemon rounds. Spoon mushrooms over the lemons. May also be used as a salad dressing with greens and tomatoes or a marinade for artichoke hearts.

MUSTARD SALAD DRESSING

2 tablespoons white wine vinegar
2 tablespoons Dijon mustard
1 cup olive oil or salad oil
salt and pepper, to taste

Mix vinegar and mustard together; slowly add oil and whisk until blended.

REBID JELLO SALAD

6 ounce package lime jello
1 13 1/2-ounce can crushed pineapple
1 pint small curd cottage cheese
1 cup mayonnaise

Add enough boiling water to drained pineapple juice to make 4 cups and add to jello. When jello is thickened, add other ingredients and put all in blender.

GREEK SALAD

1 head Romaine lettuce
2 medium tomatoes, cut into wedges
1 cucumber, sliced
4 green onions, sliced
3 radishes, sliced
8 ounces feta cheese, crumbled
1/4 cup Greek black olives
1 1/2 teaspoons finely chopped fresh
  mint
1/2 cup olive oil
1/4 cup lemon juice
2 tablespoons red wine vinegar
1 clove garlic, minced
1/2 teaspoon chopped fresh oregano

Place lettuce, tomatoes, cucumber, radishes, green onions, cheese and olives in salad bowl. Blend the remaining ingredients and pour over salad and toss.

HONEY-LIME DRESSING FOR FRUIT SALAD

3/4 cup salad oil
1/3 cup honey
1/4 cup lime juice
2 tablespoons lemon juice
1/4 teaspoon dry mustard
1/2 teaspoon paprika
2 tablespoons toasted sesame seeds

Combine and beat. Good on pineapple, strawberries, green grapes, papaya, oranges, bananas, and peaches. Toss fruit with dressing and serve on lettuce.

FRESH BASIL VINAIGRETTE

4 tomatoes
1 onion
1/2 cup light olive oil
splash red-wine vinegar
2 sprigs chopped fresh basil
salt and pepper to taste

Cut tomatoes and onion in slices. Combine oil, vinegar, basil, salt, pepper and shake and drizzle over tomatoes and onion.

OVERCALL ORANGE VINAIGRETTE

2 tablespoons orange juice
1 tablespoon red wine vinegar
1 teaspoon Dijon mustard
1/2 teaspoon grated orange peel
salt and pepper to taste
2 tablespoons olive oil

Blend in blender. Good on vegetable salads and asparagus.

LEMON VINAIGRETTE

2 tablespoons lemon juice
1 1/2 teaspoons mustard
1 tablespoon oil
1/4 cup water
2 tablespoons diced green pepper
2 tablespoons diced red pepper
2 tablespoons diced radishes
2 green onions, diced
1 tablespoon chives

Great for vegetables.

PASS

BREADS

MRS. J'S WALNUT BREAD LOAF

Makes 1 loaf

1 1/2 cups sugar
1/2 cup butter
2 egg yolks
1 cup mashed bananas
1 cup sour milk
2 1/2 cups white flour
1 1/2 teaspoons soda
1/2 teaspoon salt
1 teaspoon vanilla
1/2 cup nuts

Cream butter and sugar. Add beaten egg yolks and bananas. Continue beating; add dry ingredients and milk alternately. Add vanilla and nuts. Bake in loaf pan at 375° for 45 minutes.

STRAWBERRY NUT BREAD

Makes 2 loaves

1/2 cup shortening
1 1/2 cups sugar
3 eggs
1 1/2 cups strawberries, mashed
4 cups flour
1 1/2 teaspoons soda
1 1/2 teaspoons baking powder
1/2 teaspoon salt
1/2 cup sour cream
2 teaspoons vanilla
1 cup chopped walnuts

Cream shortening and sugar; add eggs, beat well and add strawberries. Add dry ingredients to creamed mixture, alternately with sour cream. Blend and add vanilla and walnuts. Pour into 2 greased loaf pans. Bake at 350° for 60 minutes. Remove from pan and cool on racks.

SCONES

1 cup self-rising flour
1 stick softened butter
2 tablespoons sugar
4-5 tablespoons milk
1 lightly beaten egg
pinch salt

Sift flour and salt, cut in butter; add sugar and 4 tablespoons milk. Turn on floured surface and knead 10 times. Form in ball; roll out to 3/4″ thickness and cut out in 2″ rounds. Brush tops with beaten eggs and place on greased baking sheet. Bake 12-15 minutes at 425°.

CHEESE GARLIC BREAD
Serves 8

Cut off sides and top crusts from unsliced white bread — leave bottom. Slice 8 thick slices (from a small loaf) not clear through the button, the length of the loaf.

Mix together:
1/4 pound butter or margarine
2 cloves minced garlic
1/2 pound sharp cheddar cheese

Spread between slices, on top and sides. Heat oven to 300° and cook for 25 minutes.

CHEESY BREAD

1 loaf French bread
1/2 pound margarine
1/8 pound Romano cheese, grated
1/2 teaspoon Worcestershire sauce
1/4 pound cheddar cheese, grated
1/4 teaspoon garlic salt

Mix ingredients. Toast one side of French bread, and then spread mixture on other side and put under broiler until bubbly.

BRENT'S CHRISTMAS CAKE

1/2 pound margarine
2 cups sugar
2 eggs
1/2 teaspoon vanilla
1 cup sour cream
1 3/4 cups flour
1 teaspoon baking powder
1/4 teaspoon salt
1/2 cup chopped walnuts or pecans
2 teaspoons dark brown sugar
1 1/2 teapoons cinnamon

Heat oven to 350°. Butter 10″ tube pan. Cream butter and sugar; add eggs, then vanilla and sour cream. Add flour, baking powder and salt. Spoon half of mixture in pan; sprinkle with half of nut-brown sugar mixture. Cover with rest of batter, then remaining nut mixture. Bake 1 hour. Cool in pan on rack. When cool remove and turn over on plate. The neighbors love this for their Christmas morning breakfast — a tradition in our family and theirs started by our son, many years ago.

WICHITA PECAN ROLLS

1 package frozen rolls
1/2 cup brown sugar
1/2 stick butter
1/2 cup chopped pecans

Melt brown sugar, butter and pecans in bottom of 9″ x 13″ pan.

Melt together:
1 cup white sugar
1 stick butter
1 tablespoon cinnamon

Coat rolls with mixture of white sugar, butter and cinnamon and place in pan. Cover lightly with wax paper and let rise overnight. Bake 30 minutes in oven at 350°. Let stand 10 minutes. Turn out on platter or pan with a rim.

GRAND SLAM

DESSERTS

FRUIT PIZZA

Make either a filbert or other nut pie crust using 1 1/2 cups ground nuts, 3 tablespoons granulated sugar, 1/4 cup soft butter. (A gingersnap cookie crumb crust or vanilla wafer crumbs crust will do also.) Press mixture in a 11″ pizza pan.

Filling: 1 12-ounce package softened cream cheese, 1/4 cup granulated sugar, 1 teaspoon vanilla. Mix and spread over crust. Arrange fruit in circular pattern over cream cheese filling. Use any fruit, canned or fresh, on top of filling. Do not use frozen. Strawberries and kiwis are pretty, also blueberries. Glaze the fruit with 1/2 cup apricot preserves, or 1/2 cup orange marmalade mixed with 2 tablespoons of water and heated. Keep refrigerated until needed.

STRAWBERRY RING

Serves 8

Whip 3 pints softened lemon sherbert with 1/3 cup creme de menthe. Mold and freeze. Fill center with whole strawberries.

STRAWBERRY PIE

Serves 6

1 cooked pie shell
1 1/2 quarts fresh strawberries
1/2 cup water
1 cup sugar
2 1/2 teaspoons cornstarch

Wash and hull strawberries. Place 1 quart of berries in pastry shell. Crush 1/2 quart berries and combine with water, sugar and cornstarch in a saucepan. Boil for 2 minutes or until clear. Spoon glaze over all the berries. Cool. Can be served with whipped cream. Our boys could hardly wait for summer and Hope's Strawberry Pie.

STRAWBERRIES ROMANOFF

1 quart strawberries
1/4 cup Grand Marnier
2 tablespoons Confectioner's sugar
1 pint vanilla ice cream
1/2 pint whipped cream

Combine halved strawberries, Grand Marnier and sugar. Refrigerate several hours. Before serving, soften ice cream. Whip cream; combine with ice cream and strawberry mixture. Garnish with whole strawberries. Hoppie's Vic introduced me to Strawberries Romanoff — special man, special memories.

CHOCOLATE DIPPED KABOBS

1 cup semisweet chocolate mini chips
1 teaspoon shortening (not butter or margarine)

Combine in top of double boiler; place over water, and stir until melted. Cool slightly before dipping fruit. Refrigerate fruit until chocolate is firm. Strawberries with stems, cherries with stems, kiwi fruit, bananas and half a cookie are good for dipping. Perfect dessert for a shower.

AN ANGEL OF AN ANGEL PIE

6 egg whites
1/2 teaspoon cream of tartar
1/4 teaspoon salt
3/4 cup sugar
1 teaspoon vanilla
maple flavoring
ground nuts

Beat egg whites until foamy; add cream of tartar and salt and continue beating until stiff enough to stand in peaks. Fold in sugar and vanilla. Bake in ungreased 8″ or 9″ pie pan at 325° for 20 minutes. When cool and not long before serving, add 1/2 pint cream whipped with 1/2 cup sugar and maple flavoring and cover with ground nuts. Black walnuts are best. This is a favorite in our family and one my mother made for very special occasions and her bridge club. An old family recipe.

THE PEPPERMINT TWIST

Serves 8

3/4 cup butter
1 cup sugar
3 eggs
3 ounces melted chocolate (cooled)
1/2 teaspoon peppermint flavoring

Cream butter and sugar. Add eggs, cooled melted chocolate and flavoring and beat well. May be put in graham cracker crust and topped with crumbs, or crust may be omitted. Refrigerate 6 hours. Keeps 2-3 days in refrigerator.

CHOCOLATE ANGEL CAKE DESSERT

Serves 10-12

1 12-ounce package chocolate chips
1 tablespoon sugar
3 eggs, separated
2 cups whipping cream
1 teaspoon vanilla
1 cup slivered almonds, toasted
1 Angel food cake
1/4 cup Kahlua

Melt chocolate chips in top of double boiler and add sugar. Beat egg yolks and add to chocolate. Remove from heat and cool 5 minutes. Beat egg whites until stiff and fold into chocolate mixture. Add whipped cream, vanilla, Kahlua, and almonds. Cut top off cake and hollow out inside, leaving 1″ sides and bottom. Fill with mixture, leaving enough to ice the cake after top has been put back on. Refrigerate overnight.

CHEESE PIE

Serves 10-12

2 cups graham cracker crumbs
1/2 cup sugar
1/2 cup melted butter

Mix first 3 ingredients and press into a 9" springform pan.

8 ounces cream cheese, softened
2 eggs
2/3 cup sugar
1 teaspoon vanilla

Blend cream cheese, eggs, sugar and vanilla and pour into crust. Bake at 375° for 20 minutes. Remove from oven; let pie stand for 15 minutes.

1 cup sour cream
2 tablespoons sugar
1 teaspoon vanilla

Combine sour cream, sugar and vanilla and spread over baked filling. Return pie to a 425° oven and bake 10 minutes. Cool and chill overnight before serving. Can garnish with fresh berries.

OZARK TWO-BID PUDDING

Serves 6

1 egg
3/4 cup sugar
1 1/4 teaspoons baking powder
1/8 teaspoon salt
1/2 cup chopped apple
1/2 cup chopped nuts
1 teaspoon vanilla
2 tablespoons flour

Beat egg and sugar together until smooth. Add flour, baking powder, salt to egg mixture. Add nuts, apples and vanilla. Bake in a greased pie tin at 325° for 35-40 minutes. Serve hot or cold with cream or ice cream. This was always called Bess Truman's dessert in the midwest.

DESSERT WHEN YOU FORGOT

**Dash to Safeway and buy one Angel
  food cake at the bakery
2 pints of strawberries
1 pint of whipping cream**

At home again, cut off the top of the cake about an inch from the top and hollow out, leaving an inch on sides and bottom. Whip cream and add sliced strawberries. Add sugar if you have a sweet tooth. Fill cake, leaving enough of the whipped cream mix to frost the cake. Refrigerate until serving time.

If you had thought about dessert earlier you can make a meringue and put the strawberries and whipped cream in it.

**Meringue:
3 egg whites
1/4 teaspoon cream of tartar
1 cup sugar**

Beat egg whites until stiff and glossy, adding cream of tartar and sugar gradually. Place a greased sheet of foil on a cookie sheet. Spread meringue on foil and shape into 11″ shell. Bake for 1 1/2 hours at 275°. Turn off oven and leave meringue in oven for at least another 2 hours. When cool, fill with strawberry mixture. Chill another 2 hours.

PEACHES AND CRÈME FRAICHE

Serves 1

1 fully ripe peach, peeled, halved and seeded, per serving
2 tablespoons Crème Fraiche
1/4 cup raspberries, blackberries or blueberries

Top each peach half with a tablespoon of Creme Fraiche and sprinkle with berries.

CRÈME FRAICHE

1 cup heavy cream
1 tablespoon plain yogurt, buttermilk or sour cream

Heat cream until lukewarm. Remove from heat, stir in yogurt and pour into a glass jar with screwtop lid. Let stand at room temperature 8 hours or overnight. (Cream will thicken slightly.) Do not stir. Refrigerate, covered tightly, for up to one week. Makes 1 cup.

MUD PIE

Serves 8-10

1 1/2 cups chocolate wafer crumbs
6 tablespoons margarine
1 quart coffee ice cream, slightly softened
chocolate fudge sauce
whipped cream
toasted almonds

Combine cookie crumbs with melted margarine and press into a 9″ pie pan on bottom and sides. Fill with softened ice cream. Top with fudge sauce and freeze until firm. Garnish with whipped cream and toasted almonds. (When making the crumb crust, press into place by placing another pie pan on top of the crumbs and pressing them into place.)

GRAND SLAM FROZEN CHOCOLATE DESSERT

Serves 18

1 cup butter or margarine
2 cups sifted powdered sugar
4 squares unsweetened melted
  chocolate
4 eggs
3/4 teaspoon peppermint flavoring
2 teaspoons vanilla
1 cup vanilla wafer crumbs

Beat butter and powdered sugar until light and fluffy. Add melted chocolate. Add eggs and flavorings. Sprinkle 1/2 of the crumbs in each of 18 cupcake pan liners. Spoon in chocolate. Top with remaining crumbs. Freeze. Garnish top if desired.

KANSAS'S CHERRY COBBLER

Serves 6

3/4 cup flour
1 1/2 teaspoons baking powder
pinch salt
2 tablespoons fat
1/3 cup milk

Mix flour, baking powder and salt. Cut in fat with knife or blender and slowly add milk. Place soft dough over cherries.

2 cups seeded fresh cherries (or 1 #2
  can)
2/3 cup sugar
1 tablespoon flour
1/4 teaspoon nutmeg
1/2 cup water (if you use fresh
  cherries)
2 tablespoons butter

Blend chereries, sugar, flour and nutmeg. Pour into buttered baking dish. Dot top with butter. Put the dough on top by spoonfuls. Bake at 350° for 25 minutes. Can use other berries.

INDEX

ACES

FINESSE

GRAND SLAM
2356 Cascade Way
Longview, Wash. 98632

Please send me _____ copies of **GRAND SLAM** @ $10.60 ea. _____
Plus postage and handling @ $1.75 ea. _____
(Washington residents add applicable tax to cost of book) _____
TOTAL _____

Enclosed is my check ☐ or money order ☐
Make checks payable to **GRAND SLAM**

PLEASE PRINT OR TYPE

NAME _____

ADDRESS _____

CITY _____ STATE _____ ZIP _____

GRAND SLAM
2356 Cascade Way
Longview, Wash. 98632

Please send me _____ copies of **GRAND SLAM** @ $10.60 ea. _____
Plus postage and handling @ $1.75 ea. _____
(Washington residents add applicable tax to cost of book) _____
TOTAL _____

Enclosed is my check ☐ or money order ☐
Make checks payable to **GRAND SLAM**

PLEASE PRINT OR TYPE

NAME _____

ADDRESS _____

CITY _____ STATE _____ ZIP _____

GRAND SLAM
2356 Cascade Way
Longview, Wash. 98632

Please send me _____ copies of **GRAND SLAM** @ $10.60 ea. _____
Plus postage and handling @ $1.75 ea. _____
(Washington residents add applicable tax to cost of book) _____
TOTAL _____

Enclosed is my check ☐ or money order ☐
Make checks payable to **GRAND SLAM**

PLEASE PRINT OR TYPE

NAME _____

ADDRESS _____

CITY _____ STATE _____ ZIP _____